To really appreciate the work
the political and cultural cont
Humankind needed Shelley back then, and this book reminds us of how
much we need him now. It is an honest, straightforward, revolutionary look
at a truly revolutionary life. The world needs more Shelley, the world needs
this book.

Benjamin Zephaniah

Fresh, clear and compelling, this is the best compact account of Percy Bysshe
Shelley's revolutionary life currently available. Jacqueline Mulhallen places
Shelley vividly in his own times, and shows how and why his imagination,
vision and new exciting art offer such inspiring examples to us now.

Nicholas Roe, Professor of English Literature,
University of St Andrews

In this compelling and eye-opening study, Jacqueline Mulhallen demonstrates
how Percy Bysshe Shelley's passionate humanitarianism enlightens every
aspect of the revolutionary agenda that informs all his writing, poetry and
prose alike. Thoroughly researched and engagingly written, Mulhallen's
book reminds us anew of that great Romantic's robust socio-political vision,
a vision that remains as relevant and vital for our own volatile times as it was
for his some two centuries ago – if not even more so.

Stephen C. Behrendt, George Holmes
Distinguished Professor of English, University of Nebraska

Full of suggestive insights and highly readable, this is an absorbing study
of Shelley's life, thought, and writing. Jacqueline Mulhallen has written a
valuable book; she is especially good on Shelley's revolutionary significance.

Michael O'Neill, Professor of English, Durham University

This book provides a fresh and impassioned account of the significance
of Shelley's radical life and writings. It handles an array of historical and
biographical contexts with clarity and skill, and takes on board the findings
of recent scholarship. A fine and highly readable achievement.

Michael Rossington, Professor of Romantic Literature,
Newcastle University

Percy Bysshe Shelley

Revolutionary Lives

Series Editors: Sarah Irving, University of Edinburgh;
Professor Paul Le Blanc, La Roche College, Pittsburgh

Revolutionary Lives is a series of short, critical biographies of radical figures from throughout history. The books are sympathetic but not sycophantic, and the intention is to present a balanced and, where necessary, critical evaluation of the individual's place in their political field, putting their actions and achievements in context and exploring issues raised by their lives, such as the use or rejection of violence, nationalism, or gender in political activism. While individuals are the subject of the books, their personal lives are dealt with lightly except insofar as they mesh with political concerns. The focus is on the contribution these revolutionaries made to history, an examination of how far they achieved their aims in improving the lives of the oppressed and exploited, and how they can continue to be an inspiration for many today.

Also available:

Salvador Allende:
Revolutionary Democrat
Victor Figueroa Clark

Sylvia Pankhurst:
Suffragette, Socialist and Scourge of Empire
Katherine Connelly

Hugo Chávez:
Socialist for the Twenty-first Century
Mike Gonzalez

Paul Robeson:
A Revolutionary Life
Gerald Horne

Frantz Fanon
Philosopher of the Barricades
Peter Hudis

Ellen Wilkinson:
From Red Suffragist to Government Minister
Paula Bartley

Leila Khaled:
Icon of Palestinian Liberation
Sarah Irvin

Gerrard Winstanley:
The Digger's Life and Legacy
John Gurney

Jean Paul Marat:
Tribune of the French Revolution
Clifford D. Conner

www.revolutionarylives.co.uk

Percy Bysshe Shelley

Poet and Revolutionary

Jacqueline Mulhallen

PlutoPress
www.plutobooks.com

First published 2015 by Pluto Press
345 Archway Road, London N6 5AA

www.plutobooks.com

British Library Cataloguing in Publication Data
A catalogue record for this book is available from the British Library

ISBN   978 0 7453 3462 2   Hardback
ISBN   978 0 7453 3461 5   Paperback
ISBN   978 1 7837 1702 6   PDF eBook
ISBN   978 1 7837 1704 0   Kindle eBook
ISBN   978 1 7837 1703 3   EPUB eBook

This book is printed on paper suitable for recycling and made from fully
managed and sustained forest sources. Logging, pulping and manufacturing
processes are expected to conform to the environmental standards of the
country of origin.

Typeset by Stanford DTP Services, Northampton, England
Text design by Melanie Patrick
Simultaneously printed by CPI Antony Rowe, Chippenham, UK
and Edwards Bros in the United States of America

To William Alderson and Dritan Dauti

Contents

Acknowledgements		x
Prologue		xii

1. Shelley's Family Background and Education: 1792–1811   1
2. The Lake District, Ireland and Devon: 1811–13   26
3. *Tremadog, Queen Mab* and the 'Hermit of Marlow': 1813–18   52
4. Italy and Shelley's Annus Mirabilis: 1818–19   80
5. Satire and Drama: 1819–22   103
6. The Legacy of a Revolutionary   128

Notes   137
Index   155

Acknowledgements

Firstly, many thanks to Alex Snowdon for suggesting that I write an article about Shelley for www.counterfire.org and to Neil Faulkner for suggesting that I develop this article into a book and for continuing to encourage me. Many thanks, too, to Nicholas Roe, Peter Vassallo and Ivan Callus for inviting me to read a paper on Shelley's reform pamphlets at the wonderful 2014 *Encountering Malta* conference, and Peter Vassallo for subsequent advice. I would also like to thank those at the September 2013 'William Cobbett at 250 Colloquium' at Nuffield College, Oxford, where I had helpful discussions on Shelley, Spence and Cobbett, especially with John Gardner and Malcolm Chase.

I am very grateful to Jeremy Knight, Curator of Horsham Museum, for sharing with me new information about Timothy Shelley's parliamentary career, and to Brian Alderson for telling me about the Godwins and children's publishing and showing me the books in his collection.

I want to thank Dominic Alexander and John Gardner for reading chapters of the book and for their very helpful comments and Nora Crook for reading nearly all of it in a very short time and giving me excellent advice. I also thank William Alderson, my husband, for patiently reading complete drafts many times and making useful suggestions.

There would have been no illustrations without the kind help of my friends. John Gardner sent me a copy of his own print of *The Radical Ladder*, Angus Graham-Campbell permitted William to photograph his copy of *Eton Sketched* and showed us both round Eton College, including a visit to the Library, and Nora Crook allowed William to photograph some of the books and pamphlets in her fascinating collection. I am very grateful to John, Nora, Angus and William.

Living in a Norfolk village without public transport meant that my Carlyle membership of the London Library was invaluable. I am grateful to all the staff there but especially those in Country Orders

Department, who promptly sent me books, and Gosia Lawik very kindly answered my queries. I also thank the staff at Cambridge University Library for their help.

Thanks too to all my friends and comrades in StoptheWar nationally for following Shelley's advice about 'great assemblies' and, locally, to those in King's Lynn and Wisbech StoptheWar. In Wisbech the tradition of protesting against racism, war and attacks on workers continues under the Thomas Clarkson Memorial.

Thanks to David Castle who gave me crucial advice, to Robert Webb, Emily Orford and all at Pluto Press who have been working on this book, and to the anonymous readers of my proposal who gave me such very encouraging feedback.

Finally, I would like to especially thank William, who encouraged my writing another book about Shelley, helped with computer difficulties and compiled the index (needless to say, any mistakes are mine alone). He gave time which he could have spent on his own innumerable interests, including writing his fine poetry, in order to give me the time I needed to complete the book. Thanks just doesn't cover my appreciation of what he has done. I would like to think I could repay him, but I owe him too much for that.

Prologue

It is 21 May 2015. A film opens in cinemas across the UK. It is a
documentary by Amir Amirani about the origins and consequences
of the international protest on 15 February 2003 against the Iraq
war. On every continent – even Antarctica – people demonstrated
in the largest protest the world had ever seen. Dismissed by some
with a 'Well, we didn't stop them, did we?', the protest actually
had a continuing profound influence on events across the world,
particularly in Egypt. The title of the film is *We Are Many*, and it opens
with the final stanza of *The Mask of Anarchy* by Percy Bysshe Shelley:

> Rise like lions after slumber
> In unvanquishable number.
> Shake your chains to earth like dew,
> Which in sleep had fallen on you;
> Ye are many, they are few.

Shelley's revolutionary ideas did not escape his contemporary
reviewers, and he was famously attacked in the right-wing journal
The Quarterly Review. On the other hand, his poem *Queen Mab* was
circulated so enthusiastically among radicals and the emerging
working class that it was known as 'The Chartists' Bible'. Afraid of the
influence of his ideas, critics seized on Shelley's atheism to condemn
him as a wicked man. His desertion of his first wife, Harriet, and his
desire to set up a second family with Mary Godwin, was considered
abundant confirmation of this, even though many men kept mistresses
and visited prostitutes without challenge. Even today, when he is
less likely to be attacked for his atheism, his love-life and financial
difficulties are used to undermine him and his revolutionary ideas.
His bicentenary brought diatribes as well as varying degrees of praise.

Despite the international fame he gave to 'We are many, they
are few', Shelley is still seen by some left-wing commentators as
being politically and poetically negligible. They wonder whether

his poetry is too obscure to communicate to a mass audience, and whether poetry even should 'make sense' in the way prose does, or just communicate imagery and emotion like painting and music. Some writers (including those who are divorced) have accused him of sexism because he deserted his first wife. Others, like the left-wing journalist Paul Foot, have suggested that he would have been a greater political poet if he had remained in England. It is true that he might have been more successful in getting his political poetry published if he had not had to rely on others to act for him, but without his union with Mary Godwin, or his life in Italy, Shelley might never have written his greatest poems, nor Mary her famous novel, *Frankenstein*.

It is often suggested that Shelley did not sincerely wish to overthrow the system, as he was born an aristocrat. He could not easily rid himself of an aristocratic manner which embarrassed Leigh Hunt and caused Byron to describe him as 'perfect a Gentleman as ever crossed a drawing room'.[1] Although Shelley 'loved the people', he did not want to be a worker. He needed time for writing and political activity and, as he explained to Godwin, workers did not have the time or the education.[2] He tried to find a middle way, rejecting his full inheritance, sharing what money he had, and mixing with journalists, doctors and other professionals rather than aristocrats. Whilst he employed servants, he seems to have accorded them more respect than was common then – or now. For example, he took Elise Duvillard, one of the children's nursemaids, to the opera and praised the other nursemaid, Milly Shields, for her prowess in astronomy.[3]

In the 1980s three books were published about Shelley's politics: P.M.S. Dawson's *The Unacknowledged Legislator*, Paul Foot's *Red Shelley* and Michael Scrivener's *Radical Shelley*. They were all valuable and illuminating studies, but much more material has come to light since then. Dawson saw Shelley as a Foxite Whig and Godwinian whose revolution was far in the future. Scrivener and Foot connected Shelley more firmly to Thomas Paine, William Cobbett and the radicals. In fact, Shelley was also indebted to Jean-Jacques Rousseau and the French revolutionary writers, to the British empiricist philosophers, and even to John Gale Jones's British Forum and the Society of Friends (Quakers). He was very open-minded and considered political ideas from all sources, and the links between all these figures and their followers were greater, after all, as the population was so much smaller than now.

With the repressive measures of the 1790s, the United Irishmen and the London Corresponding Society members were silenced and their ideas derided by the ruling class, but within 20 years the slave trade had been abolished and the reform movement was reviving. Shelley supported these campaigns and supported people who attempted to spread education, better living conditions and techno-logical advances. He rejected the dominance of 'the few' and insisted on the need for equality, but he also opposed violence, inspiring Gandhi, and leading many to believe that he was a pacifist. These days fewer people than ever own more of the world's wealth than ever before, and Shelley's arguments about violence are still important. He reasoned that it was to be avoided if possible because its use by 'the many' might have a corrupting adverse effect because it is the weapon of 'the few' in defence of their power and inequality.

That violence has forced more and more people to desperately flee war and persecution, with Muslims in particular being attacked and their religion misrepresented in order to feed divisions. It is worth remembering that Shelley hoped that 'the Mahometan, the Jew, the Christian, the Deist, and the Atheist will live together in one community [. . .] united in the bonds of charity and brotherly love'. He would have been proud to have his poetry associated with the expression of unity in opposition to war and violence which was the demonstration of 15 February 2003. Shelley has been dead for nearly 200 years, but he was with us on that day.

1

Shelley's Family Background and Education: 1792–1811

I t may seem strange for a political biography of Shelley to begin
like a Victorian novel by asserting that its hero was a gentleman
from an old, distinguished family, but this fact clearly makes a
difference to Shelley's enemies. They state that he was not, and
therefore when he rebelled against the aristocratic, landowning class
it hardly mattered, since he was *nouveau riche* and so never really of
that class.[1] The Shelley family, however, dated back to the eleventh
century, included a Knight of Malta and Catholic martyrs, and was
connected by marriage to most of the prominent families in Sussex.
Shelley's great-grandfather was a third son who had emigrated
to America, but he sent Bysshe, his second son named after his
grandmother, Hellen Bysshe, back to England to be brought up by
his grandparents. Bysshe Shelley inherited property from them and
when his uncles and his own elder brother died he inherited their
estates too. He increased his property by marrying wealthy heiresses.
Bysshe had four children by his first marriage and seven by his
second, but most of the estate was to go to his eldest son, Timothy,
and was intended to be eventually inherited by Timothy's eldest son,
our hero, Percy Bysshe Shelley. Within twelve days of the birth of this
heir on 4 August, 1792, Bysshe had had his fourth child by his 'dear
friend', Eleanor Nicholls. He remarked, 'Ran Tim Damned hard Age
Considered'. He was 61, and regarded a very handsome man.[2]

His grandson said of him, 'He has acted very ill to three wives. He
is a bad man.'[3] Percy Bysshe Shelley made no distinction between
the women his grandfather married legally and Eleanor Nicholls,
whom he did not marry. His own father, Timothy, had an illegitimate
son not much older than his legitimate son and heir, Percy Bysshe

Shelley. Percy Bysshe would inevitably have seen the hypocrisy when Timothy told him that 'he would provide for as many natural children as he chose to get, but that he would never forgive his making a *mésalliance*'.[4] It was not an unusual attitude in the upper classes of the eighteenth century: marriages were usually made not for love but to unite estates. No woman had much control over important aspects of her life, including marriage; it was important for well-off families to be able to control women's marriages so that properties could be thus united. An upper-class woman, if she did not marry, with few exceptions, remained at home with no career or independent social life and certainly no sex life. Women rarely had much education and if they had any the only work they were likely to find would be as a governess. A woman from a rich family was often left in poverty after her male relative died, and women had no right to keep either inheritance or earnings if they married. Divorce was extremely rare and required an Act of Parliament: desertion was not grounds. A man could divorce his wife for adultery but a woman could not divorce her husband without evidence of exceptional brutality. If she left, she lost all rights to her children. Most people had a vicious attitude towards those women who lived independent lives or who broke the conventions of marriage, although men got away with it. Although there was no organised movement, women were increasingly demanding the right to be educated, to choose their husband and to work as they wished. Some women, such as Mary Wollstonecraft who wrote the influential *A Vindication of the Rights of Woman* in 1792, had successful lives as writers.

Field Place, an old manor house, was developed in the eighteenth century into a spacious residence with large grounds, woods and fields. Horsham, near Gatwick Airport and the M25, now has numerous large offices smothering what was in Shelley's time a pretty market town, close to the ports and a prosperous centre for 'agriculture and its associated industries, like tanning and brewing'. It had good roads to London, at least one theatre, bookshops, banks and legal offices, even a model gaol. Shelley's family patronised the local theatre and events such as May Day, celebrated with children's dancing, garlands of flowers and 'Jack in the Green', or fairs with roundabouts, shooting galleries and a Fat Lady or Living Skeleton. Similar families in the area included an Indian lady, Mrs Beauclerk, a stepsister of the United Irishman Lord Edward Fitzgerald, and French émigrés who had fled the Revolution.[5]

The French Revolution

The French Revolution was a defining event and shaped the world in which Shelley grew up. It had succeeded initially because the bourgeois class had allied against the aristocracy with the working people and were supported by the peasants, who destroyed chateaux across the country. On 14 July 1789 insurgents stormed the Bastille.[6] But the bourgeoisie wanted to stabilise the country whereas working people wanted to continue the revolution until they gained political rights, higher wages or cheaper food. When Louis XVI attempted to leave the country to obtain military help from Austria to restore his powers, the French Assembly sentenced him to the guillotine as a traitor. After his trial and execution, the Girondins, who had held power, were purged from the Assembly by the Jacobins, who more overtly courted working people. Their 1793 Constitution provided universal male suffrage and some control over representatives, but France was at war and instead of the Constitution, people got the Committee of Public Safety. The Jacobins succeeded militarily against the invading English and Austrian forces and put down a royalist rebellion, but they introduced a huge wage cut, attacked popular working men's clubs and silenced their presses. In 1795, popular insurrections calling for the Constitution of 1793 were brutally put down, one by General Napoleon Bonaparte, one of the new officers who had replaced aristocrats in the army. 'Gracchus' Babeuf, editor of the popular *Tribune of the People*, launched a 'Conspiracy of Equals' based on a plan for common ownership. There had been so many defeats that people failed to respond and the leaders were captured and executed in 1797, but in the wake of this the Jacobins revived and so did the royalists. In danger from both, the Directory turned to Bonaparte for support. He took over and continued as dictator with a war of conquest.[7]

In Britain

The French Revolution was initially welcomed by the British ruling class. Charles James Fox, the prominent Whig, said, 'How much the greatest event it is that ever happened in the world, and how much the best' and even as late as 1792 William Pitt, the Tory Prime Minister, believed that the new France would mean there would be 15 years of peace. Both parties in Parliament, Whig and Tory, represented the rich landowners who at the time did indeed rule, even though not much more than a third of the population was employed in agriculture. Factories were still small, the workforce yet unorganised, unaware of its own strength, and factory owners had not yet established their political status.[8]

For working men, the Revolution was an inspiration. In 1792, Thomas Hardy founded the London Corresponding Society, so-called because they corresponded with groups in France as well as Manchester, Sheffield, Norwich and other English cities. It was open to any working man with a weekly penny subscription. Hardy believed that common people could make their wishes felt if, and only if, they would unite. He asked, 'Have we, who are tradesmen, shopkeepers and mechanics any right to seek to obtain a parliamentary reform?' The answer was 'Yes'.[9]

When Dr Richard Price, a Unitarian minister, expressed his view that it was right for people to resist power when it was abused and to form a government of their own choosing, Edmund Burke reacted by writing *Reflections on the Revolution in France* (1790) which was firmly against any change. The French queen, Marie Antoinette, a 'delightful vision', would be revealed as 'but a woman'. Mary Wollstonecraft, in the first reply to Burke, *A Vindication of the Rights of Men* (1790), thoroughly agreed: a queen is but a woman. Burke believed that 'learning will be cast into the mire and trodden down under the hoofs of a swinish multitude', a phrase that was to become famous and mocked among the multitude so maligned. Two radical journals were entitled *Hog's Wash* and *Pig's Meat*.[10]

The more famous reply to Burke was Thomas Paine's *Rights of Man* which sold 50,000 copies by May 1791. Paine believed that government's authority came from inherited power through conquest by 'a banditti of ruffians' and that 'the Aristocracy are not the farmers who work the land but are the mere consumers of the rent'. Paine proposed to tax the rich, remove sinecures and secure disarmament, and to provide public funds for education, maternity benefit, old age pensions – many of the reforms which were introduced in twentieth-century England and which are now being dismantled.[11]

The second part to *Rights of Man* sold 200,000 copies and was reprinted continually, circulated widely and pirated, its sales swelled by the fact that there was a warrant for Paine's arrest for publishing it. He fled to France.[12] Burke's *Reflections* and Paine's *Rights of Man* clarified the class lines which were drawn. The French Revolution was destroying the privileges of the aristocracy and monarchy and that class in England was very afraid.

The government set up a system of spies, anti-Jacobin societies and newspapers to publicise guillotining and the plight of émigrés. Effigies of Paine were burnt and 'Church and King mobs' were encouraged by the government to attack 'Jacobins'. In 1791, a Birmingham mob attacked the home of the Dissenter scientist, Joseph Priestley, wrecking his library and laboratory and forcing him into exile. People were sentenced to between 18 months and four years' imprisonment for selling *Rights of* Man, or for saying 'I am for equality and no king'.[13] At this time, prisons were privately run and Cold Bath Fields prison was notorious for the inhuman way in which the inmates were treated. The young Sir Francis Burdett visited this prison on several occasions and exposed the conditions. Prisoners were kept without food, warmth, light or cleanliness and refused visitors and writing materials. Their possessions were stolen, they were beaten up and women were prostituted. Relatives of the prisoners organised protests outside, and later became Burdett's election campaign supporters with the slogan 'No Bastille!' An enquiry was set up. Burdett also vehemently opposed the slave trade and supported Catholic Emancipation and his resulting great popularity led to his being elected MP for Middlesex in 1802.[14]

Timothy Shelley's Political Career

Timothy Shelley became an MP in 1790. He was a close associate of the Duke of Norfolk, a radical Whig close to Fox and Richard Brinsley

Sheridan. To 'win over to his party the Shelley interest', Norfolk arranged for Bysshe Shelley to become a baronet, although this did not happen until 1806, and for Timothy to have one of the two Horsham seats, a privilege for which Timothy had to pay £4,000.[15] Norfolk would have been unlikely to have accepted less from Timothy since, later, he was not willing to reduce it to less than £3,000 for Sheridan.[16] The 'Foxite' Whigs supported the campaign against the slave trade, the campaign for Parliamentary reform, Catholic Emancipation and the campaign against the Test Acts which disqualified members of religious groups outside the Church of England from taking public office. They also opposed the war with France in 1793. These were popular movements outside Parliament and they overlapped. Quakers were prominent in the movement against the slave trade and were in favour of other reforms, the General Synod of Ulster condemned the slave trade and opposed the war with France and Olaudah Equiano, the 'fluent writer and speaker' against slavery, was close to Thomas Hardy, leader of the London Corresponding Society (LCS). Both the LCS and John Cartwright, the campaigner for Reform of Parliament, wholeheartedly supported the 1798 Irish Rising.[17]

Britain's slave merchants had become very rich and powerful on the profits of the 2.5 million Africans they bought and sold between 1630 and 1807 while 'it was taken for granted than one transported African in three, at least, would die of dysentery or commit suicide' within the three years.[18] Although some of the 20,000 black people in eighteenth-century England became distinguished figures, many were still slaves. They themselves began the movement for abolition because they repeatedly ran away. Working people sympathised with them – as the magistrate, John Fielding, said, 'they have the mob on their side'. Black people were in court to see the legal victory of James Somerset, when it was ruled that a slave could not be forced to leave England against his will. It was celebrated with a ball in a Westminster pub.[19] The Quakers set up a committee to campaign against the slave trade and their 1783 petitioning of Parliament was the first large-scale use of petitions. They published Thomas Clarkson's prize-winning *Essay on Slavery* and encouraged Josiah Wedgwood to produce the logo of the movement 'Am I not a Man and a Brother'. They introduced a boycott of sugar which involved many women. The Quaker printer James Phillips published the horrifying print of the section of the slave ship showing how slaves were packed in. Parliament was full of people with West Indian properties who did not want to see the slave trade abandoned, but the Prime Minister, William Pitt, did. He encouraged William Wilberforce to be its Parliamentary spokesman and to introduce an anti-slave trade bill in 1792.[20]

In Horsham there was a strong, active Quaker group and great anger against the slave trade, but Horsham was a 'rotten borough' controlled by a Lady Irwin. At that time, large towns such as Manchester and Birmingham had no Parliamentary representative while a tiny village could return two members. 'Rotten boroughs' were owned by one person and in some cases, many in Cornwall, they were owned by the Crown. Others regularly went on the market, and the MP represented no one at all in some, such as Old Sarum where the town was 'a thornbush'.[21] One of Irwin's candidates was a retired West Indian merchant and slave owner, James Baillie, so Norfolk used this corrupt system to get candidates elected to Parliament who would vote for Wilberforce's bill. Thomas Charles Medwin, the Duke of Norfolk's steward, and his colleagues bought up enough property to get control from Irwin. She successfully petitioned against the result when Norfolk's candidates were elected. Medwin was charged with 'making a false return' and Timothy lost his seat on 8 March 1792. Baillie became MP and when, on 2 April, the abolition bill was debated, he spoke against it. Even with the huge backing of public opinion, the bill was defeated. By 1792, it 'smelt of revolutionary democracy'.[22]

Norfolk dined with the Shelleys on 15 April, and the connection continued. Timothy was to become MP for New Shoreham, another seat belonging to Norfolk, in 1802 and remained so until 1817. He worked for the Sussex interest in promoting a bill to re-open the road which is now the A29, but he voted consistently against Catholic Emancipation perhaps at the wish of his electorate. He still claimed to be a reformer in 1835 when, at the age of 82, he opposed the reform candidate and former political associate, Robert Henry Hurst. In 1810 Norfolk regained the Horsham seats.[23]

Reform of Parliament

Timothy Shelley's experience illustrates why reform of Parliament became such an important and popular issue during the lifetime of his son, even though some boroughs were more democratic than Horsham. The City of London was 'solidly Whig and even at times Radical, in a political sense' and the Westminster electorate was really representative since the system of local taxes gave artisans the vote. Certain other towns and cities, such as Norwich, Bristol and Liverpool, also had a comparatively wide franchise. Preston, which elected the famous reform campaigner, Henry 'Orator' Hunt, in 1830, had virtually universal suffrage.[24] But candidates were expected to give dinners and breakfasts for the voters and distribute food, drink or money to the crowd and votes were exchanged for bribes and promises. There was no secret ballot. Voters had to pass through a crowd of men, often drunk and violent, hired by the candidates to give their name and say who they were voting for so would often vote to please their landlord. There was real mud-slinging – unsuccessful candidates were often pelted with mud while the winner was carried around the town in a chair by his supporters.[25]

Cartwright, a naval officer who had refused to serve on the British side in the American War of Independence because he agreed with the Americans, published a pamphlet demanding annual Parliaments, universal suffrage, the ballot, equal representation and payment of members – all of which the Chartists were still demanding in the 1840s and most of which were not granted until the twentieth century. He toured the country collecting signatures for a giant petition presented to Parliament on rollers – a tactic later used by women suffragists. Reform societies were formed, notably in Yorkshire, and in 1780 a committee of Westminster electors circulated a report calling for Cartwright's programme and Pitt introduced a reform bill. Further bills followed, and that of 1784 lost by only 70 votes. In 1788, a new reform campaign began, holding that freedom of conscience, of the press and election were inviolable rights. The argument against this was that having property ensured an 'independent' Parliamentary candidate and gave you a 'stake' in the country and that an MP was the 'virtual' representative of all those who did not vote. But by 1793, England and France were at war and this ensured that Lord Grey's 1793 Reform Bill was hugely defeated.[26]

Opposition to the war caused a Whig split and the 'Foxite' Whigs seceded from Parliament, although Sheridan remained because of the cause of Ireland. Association with the French was automatically a crime. In December 1792, the leaders of a Convention of Scottish reformers held in Edinburgh were arrested and were sentenced to transportation to Australia for between seven and 14 years, in effect, a death sentence for nearly all of them. Such was the bias of Lord Braxfield, who prejudged the case, that some said it was not a legal sentence.[27]An LCS meeting in the Globe Tavern, which was so well attended that the floor gave way beneath the crowd, decided that if foreign troops landed or Habeas Corpus was suspended, or the right of free meeting was attacked, the LCS would call a 'convention'. The Constitution Society, more 'moderate' reformers, said they would act with the LCS. A number of LCS members, including Thomas Hardy, were arrested on a charge of treason.

Their prosecutor was John Scott, later to become Lord Eldon, who was to rule in the 1817 custody case over Shelley's children. But the LCS members had an excellent defence counsel in Thomas Erskine, there had been a public outcry about what had happened in Scotland and thanks to Fox's 1792 Libel Act, the jury had the right to make up their own minds.[28] Shortly before the trials an anonymous article appeared in the *Morning Chronicle*, a Whig paper, and was reprinted as a pamphlet pointing out that the offence committed was not treason in legal terms. The author was William Godwin, author of *An Enquiry Concerning Political Justice*, a book which argued for the ultimate equality of mankind. Despite government efforts (warrants were out for the arrest of a further 200 people), the jury acquitted the leaders and dropped charges against others.[29]

The government introduced more and more repressive measures in 1795 after food riots, great protest meetings and petitions and a demonstration at Copenhagen Fields at which Norfolk spoke. Habeas Corpus was suspended. Following the stoning of the king's coach on its way to open Parliament, the Treason Act was introduced, which extended the meaning of treason to 'imagining the king's death', and the Seditious Meetings Act which restricted the size of public meetings to 50 persons and prevented groups from hiring halls for debate or lectures. In 1799 the LCS and other groups were prohibited. To be a reformist, or a revolutionary, for the one now implied the other, was unsafe. The war with France continued, with a brief peace, until 1815.[30]

In 1798, at a birthday dinner for Fox at the Crown and Anchor Tavern, Norfolk's toast was 'Our Sovereign's health – the Majesty of the People'. He remarked that there was the same number there around Fox as there had been around George Washington at the start of the War of American Independence. As a result of this 'treasonous' statement, he lost his lord-lieutenancy and a post as colonel. Norfolk voted for Catholic Emancipation repeatedly in the House of Lords. Although he himself had turned Protestant in order to have a political career, the Norfolks were a Catholic family and his wife was Irish. In 1812, when the Prince Regent reneged on his promise to grant Catholic Emancipation, Norfolk refused the Order of the Garter. His egalitarianism, however, had limits. Revealing himself as an enemy of the poor, he enclosed land he owned in Manchester and in 1812 set about enclosing the Horsham Common. T.C. Medwin, who was married to a cousin of Timothy Shelley's wife, Elizabeth, and whose son was second cousin to and a childhood friend of the poet, helped the Horsham people to petition against this, having meanwhile fallen out with Norfolk.[31]

Shelley's Childhood

This, then, was the political background in which Shelley grew up, and it was to form his ideas and actions. However, there was not much sign of the vegetarian Shelley was to become when his mother described him, aged two in 1795, as 'Happy P.', and said, 'you never saw a fellow enjoy anything more than he does boiled partridge and bread sauce'.[32] Yet some of Shelley's later characteristics revealed themselves in childhood, such as when he repeated 'Gray's lines on the Cat and the Gold Fish' 'word for word, after once reading'.[33] When Shelley was an adult, his friends would remark on his 'singularly retentive' memory. His father's steward, Lucas, remembered his early generosity towards the poor. 'Young Bysshe was so generous that if he met with any one in distress he would give lavishly, and if he had no money with him would borrow of me'.[34] Shelley's mother's sister was married to Sir Thomas Grove who had an estate in Wiltshire. Shelley spent a holiday there in 1808 when the Assizes (court hearings) took place. It was reported that he was 'shocked at a sentence passed on a starving man who had stolen a sheep' and 'declined to go to any of the festivities [. . .] & argued hotly with his uncle or anyone who would listen to him – I think this upset Mr. Grove who was a magistrate'. The sentence may have been death or transportation.[35]

Although Shelley's observation of his sisters and their situation and expectations in life must have influenced his conclusions that women should be equal with men, the assumption that because he had four sisters he was brought up in a 'feminine atmosphere' is not really tenable. Shelley was the eldest and the younger children could not have 'babied' him or obliged him to play 'girlish' games. It was the other way round, he had to make a special visit 'to the nursery' to see them, as his sister Hellen (born 1799) remembered. He was first tutored by the vicar, 'Taffy' Edwards, and then in 1802 sent to a preparatory school, Syon House, with T.C. Medwin's son, Thomas. By the time he was in his teens, he had a separate bachelor apartment at Field Place.[36]

Hellen remembered an imaginative and high-spirited boy 'full of cheerful fun', 'passionately fond' of his younger sisters and brother (born 1806), who told them stories about an old, grey-bearded alchemist who lived in an empty room and a great tortoise who lived in Warnham Pond. His attitude seems to have been typically elder-brotherly, affectionate but bossy, sometimes thoughtlessly rough. When he carried the little one when she was tired, he warned her not to dirty his 'beautifully cut silk pantaloons'. He took his little brother, a 'dear delightful red faced brute', parachuting 'on the green' and pulled him in a little carriage – but once he accidentally overturned it into a cabbage patch.[37] He used the girls as subjects for experiments in curing their chilblains with electricity. Hellen was excused because she was frightened and Shelley encouraged her to write poetry and even had her poems printed. He got into trouble for filling a stove with inflammable liquid, went 'contemplating the stars' at night, and dressed up and – successfully – applied for a job as a gamekeeper's boy to a neighbour, Colonel Sergison. He seems to have been indulged and rather spoilt. His cheekiness is shown by a letter he wrote asking if Tom Medwin could come for a visit: 'Now I end. I am not Your obedient servant, P.B. Shelley'. He added 'Free. P.B. Shelley' imitating his father's parliamentary privilege of free post.[38]

As a new arrival at Syon House School, Shelley was 'pounced on' by 'the democracy of tyrants'. Medwin remarks, 'We all had had to pass through this ordeal' but for Shelley, 'delicately built' with 'a profusion of brown silky hair that curled naturally', and 'ignorant of' the usual games the other boys played, Syon House was 'a perfect hell'. Medwin says that he was 'not disposed to enter their wrangles and fights', but Shelley could not have always been so aloof.[39] John Rennie remembered his 'violent and extremely excitable temper [and] most violent paroxysms of rage' when he was thwarted or teased by others. W.C. Gellibrand remembers Shelley offering to do his Latin verse homework for him while he went to play. The translation read, 'I have written these little verses, but I did not make them' and poor Gellibrand got a flogging. He said he made up for it afterwards by giving Shelley a 'pummelling'.[40]

Shelley seems to have suffered as much from the schoolmaster as from the boys. He sleepwalked into Medwin's room one night and Medwin 'not then aware of the danger' of doing so, woke him up. Shelley suffered severe shock from this, and what was worse, was punished. He did not sleepwalk at school again, but had 'waking dreams'.[41] With his excellent memory, he appeared to learn without trying and was inclined to daydream and doodle in his notebook, a habit that never left him, which got him into trouble. He soon 'surpassed all his competitors' though, and had time to read a lot of Gothic novels, tales of 'bandits, murderers and haunted castles', and a fantasy novel, *Peter Wilkins*. Medwin and he went rowing on the river and across to Richmond to the theatre. Adam Walker came to give the Syon House boys lectures in astronomy and chemistry and Shelley was fascinated by chemical experiments, by the idea of other planets (perhaps inhabited) and looking through the solar microscope. Shelley may have started writing at this time; certainly he showed a

Figure 1   From *Eton Sketched* by Quis? Epoch I. The New Fellow 2. First interview with my Dame. (Photograph by William Alderson, kind permission of Angus Graham-Campbell)

Figure 2   From *Eton Sketched* by Quis? Epoch II. The Fourth Form 3. Booking the fourth form. (Photograph by William Alderson, kind permission of Angus Graham-Campbell)

liking for imaginative literature. His sister, Elizabeth, also wrote verse and was a talented artist, and they were to collaborate as teenagers.[42]

Shelley went on to Eton, where education consisted chiefly of learning Greek and Latin, mostly by rote, reading certain Latin authors, writing Latin verse 'and a smattering of divinity and geography'; otherwise, the 'life of the average Etonian [. . .] was very largely play'.[43] There is an impression that Shelley was bullied at Eton in the same way as at Syon House, but this was created by an 1848 account by W.H. Merle which is not corroborated by his contemporaries. Merle said Shelley had 'no friends' and was 'hooted, baited like a maddened bull', and had his books knocked from under his arm. An illustration of Eton life from a slightly later period shows a rite of passage boys underwent, being pelted with books when passing from the Lower School to the Upper. A second shows a boy knocking books from under another's arm and a third shows a boy being surrounded by others and booed. These seem to have been common pranks and rituals, not aimed at any particular boy, and Shelley probably had to endure them as others did. Merle, writing 40 years later and in need of money, perhaps combined them into a misremembered or exaggerated persecution story. Mary Shelley and other later friends may have believed that Shelley was talking of Eton when he was probably referring to Syon House. There is no evidence that Shelley refused to 'fag' at Eton, i.e. to act as servant to an older boy, as Mary Shelley believed.[44] Medwin states that it was not at Eton, but at Syon House, that Shelley suffered from 'tyrants and enemies'.[45]

Merle's story seems more unlikely given that Thomas Jefferson Hogg, Shelley's chief companion at Oxford, remarked that he was 'popular among his school fellows' who had presented him with 'an unusual number of books, Greek or Latin classics'.[46] The testimonies of his numerous friends given to Shelley's biographer, Edward Dowden, bear this out. Although he 'wandered alone, chiefly with a book, for hours together', they 'appreciated' him for his intelligence, gifts, and his liking for practical jokes. Edward Leslie, later a clergyman, who claimed to be Shelley's best friend, said that the two of them were suspected of putting a bulldog in the headmaster's desk; the real culprit didn't own up until 1844. A bulldog was a much more savage animal than it is today, being used for bull-baiting. Andrew Amos, who was to become a distinguished lawyer, remembered Shelley telling marvellous stories, acting plays for the younger boy in the house, and singing the songs from *Macbeth* – at the time the witches' dances and songs by Matthew Leveridge were still performed as part of the play. William Wellesley, a cousin of the Duke of Wellington, kept a copy of Shelley's *Victor and Cazire* with a warm note. Walter S. Halliday, who also became a clergyman, said that Shelley's 'lessons were child's play to him' though he needed 'especial personal super-intendence' which was not available at Eton.[47] Shelley managed to get that from James Lind, a physician to George III and friend of the astronomer William Herschel. Lind was also a scientist, interested in electricity and astronomy. He encouraged Shelley to read Godwin's *Political Justice* and to write to notable people on matters of interest. Medwin remembers Shelley reading Pliny and Lucretius, both Latin authors who questioned religion and gave a high place to nature. Adam Walker also gave lectures at Eton and Shelley continued to make electrical and chemical experiments with the inevitable accidents. 'The greatest delight Shelley experienced at Eton was from boating' and he took part in a regatta.[48]

Shelley's letters to another Eton friend, James Tisdall, show that, as well as discussing poetry, he was as keen on shooting as his father was, and he liked skating, fishing and boats. He went to balls – the Shelleys gave one at Christmas 1808 – and the theatre. He grew up expecting to take part in politics: as a boy he was encouraged by his father to make speeches with appropriate oratorical gestures.[49]

In 1806 Pitt died and a coalition of chiefly Whigs, including Fox, known as the 'Ministry of All the Talents' took office. In the Horsham election, the bailiffs returned all the candidates and Irwin's were deselected by Parliament in favour of Norfolk's pro-abolition candidates. Although there was an appeal, it was not heard until 1808, so this time Horsham was able to support the bill for the abolition of the slave trade which received royal assent on 25 March 1807. Two 'knights', country gentlemen, were elected as MPs from each county and in May there was an election for an MP for the county of Sussex which was fought almost entirely over the issue of slavery. Shelley's friend, Colonel Sergison, with T.C. Medwin as his agent, stood against John Fuller, 'whom he denounced as a slave-trader'.

Fuller's family fortune was based on West Indian sugar plantations. Anti-slavery posters were pasted up around the town, some in verse, and of 108 Horsham voters, 86 voted for Sergison. Fuller was elected, presumably by electors from other Sussex areas, but there was a petition against the result. Shelley was later to use the campaign techniques of distributing leaflets, flyposting and public meetings which suggests that he either took part or that he observed closely.[50]

When Francis Place, a former LCS member, saw the Tory Duke of Northumberland campaigning in Westminster by getting his servants to distribute bread and cheese to the crowd in 1807, he decided to organise his own campaign. The radicals, Burdett and Lord Cochrane, Place's candidates, were elected. In 1809, Burdett introduced a programme for reform: redrawing the electoral districts, extending the vote and abolishing two very unpopular institutions, sinecures and the standing army. He was seconded by William Madocks. 'The reform movement began to revive.'[51] Shelley's sister, Elizabeth, mentions 'Burdett's reformation' in a poem included in the 1810 collection that she and Shelley collaborated on, *Victor and Cazire*. Apart from 'The Irishman's Song', there are no other political references in the book but there is no doubt that Shelley admired Burdett to whom, in 1811, he dedicated *The Wandering Jew*.[52]

First Love

The Groves visited Field Place in August 1808, and Shelley and his cousin, Harriet, fell in love. Although they were only to meet a few times over the next couple of years, they kept up a regular correspondence, not discouraged by either family, who would not have disapproved of a marriage between them. Tom Medwin remembered Harriet as being 'like some Madonna of Raphael' – he never saw another woman who could compete with her for beauty. The families met in London in April 1809 and went to the opera and the theatre together. Shelley wrote proudly to Tisdall to 'observe *who* I am with'.[53]

Perhaps inspired by Harriet, Shelley now embarked on a very creative period. He wrote a novel, *Zastrozzi*, in the Gothic style, set in the Alps and in Venice, with storms, dungeons and palaces, and featuring a conniving, revengeful villain, Zastrozzi, and a dissembling murderess, Matilda, who plot to estrange the hero from his true love, Julia. *Victor and Cazire* was printed by C. and W. Phillips at Worthing with Timothy's agreement and Shelley rode over to supervise, and perhaps help with, the printing.[54] Shelley and Elizabeth collaborated again on a comedy which they sent to the famous comic actor, Charles Mathews, who returned it saying 'it wouldn't do for acting'. Shelley tried writing a tragedy, and a narrative poem, *The Wandering Jew. St Irvyne*, the novel he completed in the autumn of 1810, though similar to *Zastrozzi* in its Gothic tale and setting, expresses views against the established religion and marriage which he may have derived from Godwin's *Political Justice*. Given his generosity to the poor and sense of injustice as a child, Shelley may have been particularly receptive to Godwin's opinions. Godwin begins by emphasising the importance of education and saying that explaining and reasoning with children is a better method than beating and punishing them. Shelley was angry when he visited his sisters' school and found Hellen with a black mark hung round her neck.[55]

If Dissenters and Catholics were considered outsiders in the repressive environment of a Britain at war with Napoleonic France, atheists were viewed as even worse. Some writers rejected orthodox religion for reasons of science, radical politics and comparative mythology. Those who supported the views of Georges Cuvier, who had studied prehistoric remains and consequently did not subscribe to the accepted age of the earth, or Sir William Jones, who attempted to show the similarities between all religions, were regarded with suspicion. Burke's *Reflections* had associated freethinkers with the French Revolution, and radicals were accounted atheists and atheists radicals, although this was not necessarily the case. Most people in England were sincerely Christian. Harriet Grove's brother, Charles, and at least two of Shelley's close friends at Eton, Leslie and Halliday, were to become clergymen. Many radicals and atheists during this period either changed or concealed their views. Medwin describes Timothy Shelley as not very religious for 'although he occasionally went to the parish church, and made his servants regularly attend divine service, he possessed no true devotion himself, and inculcated none to his son'.[56]

Charles Grove remembers that in the spring of 1810 Shelley was 'full of life and spirits and very well pleased with his successful devotion to my sister', Harriet, whom he was 'more attached to [. . .] than I can express'.[57] Harriet's repeated references to 'dear Bysshe' and her hopes of visiting Field Place show that she too was sincere and she was happy when they met in April 1810. She had hurt her foot, so she managed to get two evenings at home with Shelley and her mother while the others went out.[58] According to Grove, 'she became uneasy at the tone of his letters on speculative subjects', i.e. religion, and she therefore ended the relationship, but Hellen Shelley believed that it was ended by Harriet's father.[59] Shelley, judging from his correspondence with Hogg later in the year, was not yet an atheist, although he sent Harriet a copy of John Locke's *Essay Concerning Human Understanding* and may have relayed views from *Political Justice* which were likely to alarm her family. Many of the references to Shelley's letters are heavily crossed out in her diary and she may have later wished to hide his 'speculative' remarks. The fact that her family were throwing her together with a young (and wealthy) clergyman, William Helyar, suggests that Harriet was being persuaded. She eventually married Helyar.

Shelley also sent Harriet *Victor and Cazire*, but he and Elizabeth had made a tactless mistake. Harriet's sister, Charlotte, who had been on a visit to her (and Shelley's) uncle, Captain John Pilfold, was very taken with Colonel Sergison. A verse letter from Elizabeth to Harriet included some mocking lines hoping that Sergison would fall in love with Charlotte. A young woman was not supposed to initiate a relationship and even a woman as attractive as Charlotte must have been was considered to be 'on the shelf' by her mid-20s. Elizabeth had not probably meant to be cruel, but it arrived at a particularly sad time. Harriet's younger sister, Louisa, had just died. Harriet wrote 'Charlotte offended and with reason as I think they have done very wrong in publishing what they have of her'. When Shelley's novel, *St Irvyne*, arrived, Charlotte read it and disapproved.[60]

Oxford

When Shelley went up to Oxford, he must have been very depressed, not knowing if the relationship could be healed. Norfolk was encouraging him to take up a parliamentary career, suggesting that a pragmatic view was best, and there was an agreement that Shelley would have his father's seat when he reached the age of 21. Although he must have already had doubts that he believed in them, Shelley had subscribed to the Thirty-nine Articles of the Church of England when enrolling at Oxford; an Oxford education and a career in politics would be closed to him otherwise. Godwin's view was that, as it is impossible for anyone to believe all of the Articles, a clergyman starts his career 'in duplicity and prevarication'. Shelley was not intending to be a clergyman, but he and others who wanted to take part in public life had to start their careers in the same way.[61]

Hogg suggests that Shelley might also have expressed a desire for a career in literature to Norfolk, who advised Shelley to start young in whichever career he chose. Shelley was perhaps thinking of combining the two when his father took him to the booksellers Slatter and Munday on his arrival at Oxford and said, 'my son here has a literary turn; he is already an author, and do pray indulge him in his printing freaks'. Munday published the 'very liberal' newspaper *Oxford University and City Herald* which had a wide circulation over the southern counties.[62]

Oxford was a very conservative town, which had burnt Tom Paine in effigy in 1793. At the university, the 'morose, insipid, or profligate' professors did not have to lecture, and did so rarely. Examinations were a farce. Students seldom failed and degrees were awarded on length of residence. Discipline was lax, and expulsions rare. Undergraduates went hunting, shooting and fishing and flirted with the young women of Oxford. In 1810, the *Edinburgh Review* published a series of articles attacking Oxford, complaining that 'the English clergy in whose hands education entirely rests' prevented debate upon moral and political truth in case it ended in 'religious scepticism'. Edward Coplestone, Professor of Poetry at Oxford, replied defending the Oxford stance.[63] Shelley possibly started off on the wrong side of University College. In 1809, the College had supported Lord Eldon, one of its members, in the contest for the election for Chancellor and the other members hoped for preferment through him. Shelley and his father had written to the *Morning Chronicle* supporting the Whig candidate, Lord Grenville, who was pro-Catholic Emancipation.[64]

The College might have been equally upset when Shelley supported the *Oxford Herald* in its campaign to help Peter Finnerty, formerly the editor of the United Irishmen's journal *The Press*. In 1797, a leading United Irishman, Theobald Wolfe Tone, went to France and convinced Bonaparte that France should send 14,000 troops to Ireland, but severe storms meant they could not land. The English army, however, under the instructions of Lord Castlereagh, Chief Secretary to the Lord Lieutenant, arrested and tortured 500 and executed 50. Finnerty published an article accusing Castlereagh of the brutality and citing the case of William Orr as judicial murder. Orr was convicted on the word of two Government-paid informers, and his defence counsel, John Philpot Curran, was not allowed to speak. Curran acted for Finnerty at his trial for sedition. Finnerty took the opportunity to expose Castlereagh. He was found guilty and sentenced to the pillory and two years in prison, but he said 'I can suffer anything provided it promotes the liberty of my country', and the pillory was a triumph for him. He was cheered by a large crowd and supported by leading United Irishmen, Lord Edward Fitzgerald and Arthur O'Connor (owner of *The Press*). Its printer, John Stockdale, was sentenced to six months and his press and types smashed.[65]

After his release from prison in Ireland, Finnerty, who knew Sheridan, came to England to work for the *Morning Chronicle*. In 1809, he was sent to cover the expedition ordered by Castlereagh (now Secretary of State for War) intended to block the French fleet at Antwerp. Owing to delay and incompetence on the part of the commanders, 20,000 British lives were lost, mostly from typhus on the fever marshes (the 'Walcheren disaster'). Finnerty wrote an exposé of the expedition and also referred to Castlereagh's actions in Ireland. He was sentenced to two years in Lincoln prison where he was badly treated.[66] Burdett launched a campaign in his support in London with the help of *The Examiner* and the *Oxford Herald* did the same three days later. To raise money for the *Herald*'s campaign, Shelley wrote a poem, *A Poetical Essay on the Existing State of Things*, which the newspaper published. Shelley is said to have raised £100 for Finnerty by this poem, which meant he would have sold 1,000 copies. This seems a great many but it was not impossible, given the *Oxford Herald*'s wide circulation.[67]

Shortly after he arrived, Shelley met Hogg, the son of a well-to-do Yorkshire barrister, who was considered to be a very bright student. Like Shelley, Hogg had already written a novel. Neither of them was impressed with the teaching at Oxford, and they found in each other the intellectual stimulation that the university did not provide. Although Hogg did not share Shelley's love of chemistry, he was fascinated by his description of the benefits science could bring and he remarked that Shelley read an unusual number of books, including Plato, Plutarch and Euripides in the original Greek or Latin 'without interpretation or notes'. Hogg described Shelley as a Republican and said that he had an 'inextinguishable thirst for knowledge and boundless philanthropy'.[68] At that time philanthropy meant a love of humanity and desire for equality rather than tax-deductible donations to charity while Republicans were in favour of equality and not just the abolition of the monarchy. Hogg says that many of Shelley's Eton friends were at Oxford, and they frequently called at his room for gatherings with poetry and wine. This story is confirmed by a note from Shelley to a friend, James Roe.[69] Hogg, who was later to become more conservative, writes cynically about Shelley's political views, but he may not have been so cynical at the time. He admits that 'there was no lack of beardless politicians amongst us'. Of these, 'some were more strenuous supporters of the popular cause in our little circles than others; but all were abundantly liberal'.[70]

Timothy Shelley frequently wrote to his son urging him to distinguish himself at university and to enter a poetry competition.[71] Shelley published his *Posthumous Fragments of Margaret Nicholson* edited by 'John Fitz-Victor' (the illegitimate son of the Victor of *Victor and Cazire*). Since 'imagining the death of the king' was forbidden by the 1795 Treason Act, this was a dangerous title. Margaret Nicholson was a mentally ill woman who had attempted to assassinate George III. The book included a supposed 'Epithalamium' between two more assassins: Charlotte Corday, who had stabbed the French revolutionary leader, Marat, and François Ravaillac, who had assassinated Henri IV of France. The Epithalamium contained what some believe to be a reference to oral sex. Shelley predicted that the book would sell 'like wildfire' and Hogg said it was very popular. Its political anti-war views which pinned the blame for war on monarchs could be attributed to a fictional Nicholson rather than the author. Shelley thought that no one knew who the author was, but he was wrong: at least Charles Kirkpatrick Sharpe, a graduate of Christ Church, knew, or guessed.[72]

The Necessity of Atheism

When Charles Grove came to stay over the Christmas holidays, Shelley learnt that there was no hope of his relationship with Harriet being resumed. Shelley was so distraught that his sister, Elizabeth, would follow him when he went out shooting as she was worried he might shoot himself. Shelley had hoped to invite Hogg, who had just had a broken love affair, to Field Place and introduce him to Elizabeth, but she was not interested. Anyway, his father would not allow him to. J.J. Stockdale, the publisher of *St Irvyne* (no connection to the Dublin Stockdale) had suggested to Timothy that Hogg's religious views made him an unsuitable friend for his son. But when Timothy heard from friends in the north of England that Hogg's family was 'very respectable', he invited Hogg for Easter.[73]

Shelley's letters to Hogg swerve from religion to Harriet, love and marriage and back again, showing some disturbance of mind. Shelley wrote that he was convinced of monogamy: 'A Monarchy is the only form of government (in a certain degree) which a lover ought to live under' although he added, 'I am convinced that equality will be the attendant on a more advanced & ameliorated state of society', the view Godwin expressed in *Political Justice*. He believed himself to be benefiting society by enlightening people about religion, but for this he was 'reckoned an outcast'. Although he resented Christianity as being responsible for his break with Harriet, he still believed in a 'First Cause': 'the Soul of the Universe, the intelligent & necessarily beneficent actuating principle – *This* I believe in.' He asked, 'When do we see effects without causes', a relationship which Godwin insists upon. Without this first cause 'the strongest argument in support of a future state [life after death] instantly becomes annihilated'. This correspondence began on 20 December and by 17 January 1811 Hogg had convinced him of atheism. Shelley wrote back that they now had a 'systematic cudgel' which was probably the core of the argument which he put in *The Necessity of Atheism*. Because Slatter and Munday would not publish this pamphlet, he had it printed (or printed it himself) at C. and W. Phillips.[74]

Both Shelley and Hogg were writing to clergymen, even Bishops, asking their opinion on religious matters. They hoped that the clergymen would be unable to answer their questions and they would then follow it up by sending their pamphlet. Although they wrote under pseudonyms and the correspondence had the air of the practical joke Shelley loved, Hogg insists that the enquiry was not frivolous, and certainly the discussion between the two friends was serious.[75] But because of the 1795 Seditious Meetings and Treason Acts, those who wanted to write about atheism were risking prosecution. Martin Priestman sums up the options: 'to publish and be damned; to write but not to publish; to publish under a pseudonym; and to write with enough of an air of disinterested scholarship to avoid prosecution'.[76] Hogg and Shelley appear to have been attempting to combine the last two, but as they were teenage students they were unable to carry off the final one as William Godwin had done. Shelley knew that publishing *The Necessity of Atheism* was dangerous and he wrote that he was proceeding carefully as 'we are afraid of the Legislature's powers with respect to Heretics. I was afraid that [. . .] I should be suspected as Author'.[77]

On 2 March, Shelley wrote to James Henry Leigh Hunt, editor of the radical journal *The Examiner*, to congratulate him on his acquittal on a charge of libel for publishing an article about flogging in the army. He proposed a meeting of 'enlightened and unprejudiced members of the community' to form a society to resist 'the coalition of the enemies of liberty'. This society would presumably include atheists and free thinkers and begin to fight back against the laws against libel and sedition, organised on the plan of the Illuminati, an organisation which had been successful in achieving reforms in Europe, particularly in Bavaria. Shelley had read about them in Joseph Barruel's antagonistic history with an awareness of the author's prejudice and knew that some of the Illuminati's views had influenced the United Irishmen when they were obliged to become a secret society. Shelley explained to Leigh Hunt that he would 'in all probability' have his father's seat in parliament when he was twenty-one, but that meanwhile because he was at the University 'I dare not publicly to avow all that I think, but the time will come when I hope that my every endeavour, insufficient as this may be, will be directed to the advancement of liberty'.[78] Shelley perhaps hoped to be a radical MP with the influential *Examiner* on his side, but Hunt did not reply. The letter shows that Shelley had not broken with his family or class then, and that he was well aware of the consequences of publishing *The Necessity of Atheism* under his own name.

The Necessity of Atheism is one of the earliest pamphlets on the subject to have been published in England. It argues that belief is not a voluntary act, since it is not regulated by reason and so it is a mistake to consider disbelievers to be criminals. In the absence of personal experience, it does not follow that one should believe the testimony of another who claims to have seen God, since it is possible they were deceived or mistaken, and therefore there are no proofs that there is a God. The argument that God must have created the universe is not reasonable as the universe might always have existed; if it was caused by something there is no need to assume that the cause was God.[79]

The influence of Locke's *Essay* can be seen. Hogg states that his and Shelley's reading and 'careful analysis' of this and of the arguments of David Hume was the basis for the 'little book', although it was Shelley who actually wrote it.[80] A Reverend John Walker persuaded Slatter's to burn all the copies when he saw it in the bookshop window. Hogg and Shelley had also sent copies to clergymen, professors and fellows of the colleges, including the aggressive Coplestone. Shelley later assumed that Coplestone had reported him to University College, but Shelley and Hogg were probably generally suspected. Sharpe thought they wrote it.[81] The Master of the College and 'two or three Fellows' sent for Shelley and asked him 'in a rude, abrupt and insolent tone' if he was the author. Shelley would not answer as the question was not 'just or lawful'. He was told to leave the college early the next morning. Hogg then went to the Master and Fellows and asked them to reconsider and was asked if he had written it. Hogg, later a barrister, was keen to point out that had they answered they would have either had to lie or incriminate themselves.[82]

A week or so later, Charlotte Grove noted that Shelley had been expelled from Oxford for atheism.[83] This was not so, as the college records show, but that was clearly the popular view which has persisted. Shelley, in his account of this affair to Godwin in January 1812, said that he was told that if he 'denied' it, i.e. repudiated it, 'no more would be said', but he could not do so. Hogg said this was not true, but it is suggested by Timothy Shelley's consistent attempts to get Shelley to change his opinions.[84]

Shelley and Hogg left Oxford together, though Shelley had time to say goodbye to his Eton friend, Halliday, beforehand. With this publication, Shelley had made a complete break with his old life, with his education, family and friends. The career he had planned for himself was now impossible. He probably thought he had been sufficiently cautious in his anonymity but he had reckoned without what Hogg describes as 'an affair of party'.[85] This does not mean a simple Whig–Tory rivalry, but the deep-seated hatred which the 'Church and King' party entrenched at Oxford had for anyone who questioned their views. While they turned a blind eye to drunken orgies, the College authorities had expelled two hardworking intelligent students. They and their supporters, including a Robert Clarke who reported to Hogg's father, justified their expulsion with a range of contradictory attacks on both Shelley and Hogg: they were sorry for Shelley but not Hogg or for Hogg but not Shelley. Shelley had 'always been odd' even 'suspected of insanity'; he 'dressed like a scarecrow'; both he and Hogg 'dressed differently from all others and did everything in their power to show singularity'; 'no one regretted their departure'. They also described Shelley as 'insubordinate, a ringleader in minor mischief, whose departure ensured quiet within the College'. If the last was the case, then clearly Shelley's views interested the other students: a ringleader has followers. Shelley's 'abundantly liberal' friends at Oxford clearly 'regretted his departure' – Roe would hardly have kept such an inconsequential note otherwise – and the authorities feared the influence of Hogg and Shelley over the group.[86]

2

The Lake District, Ireland and Devon: 1811–13

Four days after he and Hogg arrived in London, Shelley wrote to his father about the expulsion, trying to play it down. Timothy wrote back describing what Shelley had done as 'criminal', 'wicked' and 'diabolical'. If Shelley was to get any 'aid or assistance' from his father he had to go home immediately, not communicate with Hogg and place himself under the care of a 'gentleman as I shall appoint and attend to his instructions'.[1]

It would have been strange had Shelley and Hogg not felt loyalty towards one another after the ordeal they had just been through together. They offered counterproposals: they wanted to be able to write to each other; they offered to apologise to a correspondent; they would not publish anything on atheism or 'obtrude Atheistical opinions on anyone'; they would go home and when Hogg began his law studies, Shelley wanted to be allowed to choose a profession. Hogg's father agreed to their 'proposals', but Timothy considered them 'undutiful and disrespectful to a degree'. According to Timothy, his son had 'gloomy ideas which he has too long fix't on objects, tending to produce Temporary Insanity'. Shelley's letters suggest that he may have been suffering from stress since he entered Oxford, but it was caused by his conflict with his superiors, not by 'gloomy ideas'. The lack of sympathy or support from his father after the shock of his expulsion would have worsened this stress. Although he was usually equable and good-humoured, Shelley at times gave way to the violent rages noticed during his schooldays and he was to have a number of such rages during the coming year. If Hogg did not exaggerate, both father and son were in an emotional state when Timothy met the two of them for dinner in London.[2] The meeting was not successful.

Timothy's solicitor, William Whitton, had told him that Shelley might be prosecuted for blasphemy and, to protect himself, Timothy decided on placing his correspondence with his son in Whitton's hands. Timothy has usually been credited with being a kind-hearted man who really loved his son, but he was very quick to hand over his responsibility to someone else and remain inflexible when relatives tried to help, as John Grove did when he negotiated a £200 allowance for Shelley.[3] Shelley's statement to Godwin that his father did not feel for his welfare might well stem from this.[4]

On the other hand, John and Charles Grove were sympathetic and he spent a lot of time with them particularly after Hogg left to study law in York. They were progressive and broadminded. Hogg describes how John asked Charles, making fun of a friend for his love of the aristocracy, 'How many dukes shall we have today?' A discussion about women with other friends concluded that men and women were not unequal in intelligence although John considered they had an 'undue share of pain and sickness and suffering'. Hogg maintained that he himself claimed that 'girls learned more readily than boys, especially the mathematical sciences' while Shelley praised their 'purity, disinterestedness, generosity and kindness', suggesting that Shelley's view was idealistic and his own based on practical experience. Yet it was Shelley who had taught his sisters sciences and it would be more likely that he, not Hogg, was the one who had remarked on their aptitude.[5]

One disagreement between father and son had been over the profession Shelley had wanted to choose. Both John and Charles were studying medicine at St. Bartholomew's, John being the elder and more senior. Shelley thought he would take up surgery, but it was not considered an appropriate profession for an heir to an estate and Timothy suggested the army, which had been his own profession. Shelley later accused his father of hoping he would be 'killed in Spain' since this is where British troops had been fighting since 1808.[6] When Portugal refused to obey Bonaparte's order to close its ports to British shipping in 1807, Bonaparte had sent a punitive force via Spain but he made the mistake of putting his own brother, Joseph, on the Spanish throne. There were popular insurrections against Joseph. Spanish guerrillas had forced two divisions of the French army to surrender. When Portugal also revolted against the French, Britain seized the opportunity of sending troops under Arthur Wellesley, later Duke of Wellington. Although he had won the battle of Cintra (1809), Wellesley's greatest victories were in the future and Shelley believed this war 'a prodigal waste of human blood'.[7]

Shelley's real and lifelong concern with medicine stemmed from a serious scientific interest and a desire to help people. It may have been prompted by his friendship with Lind at Eton or arisen because he had either contracted or thought he had contracted a venereal disease while at Eton. He had undergone treatment with arsenic and other remedies, including special diets, which had undermined his health and from which he never really recovered.[8] Shelley began to attend lectures at St Bartholomew's. Here he was likely to have met William Lawrence, later to become his own physician, through Charles Grove who had a paid position as the 'box-carrier' of another eminent surgeon. Lawrence was one of the two eminent surgeons and teachers at St Bartholomew's in 1811, the very talented pupil and protégé of John Abernethy. Abernethy was a founder of hospital training, since that provided by the Royal Colleges of Physicians and Surgeons was inadequate, and Shelley respected his views on diet.[9] Lawrence differed from Abernethy on one important issue in what was described as 'the vitality debate'; i.e. what it was that made the difference between a living and a dead body. Abernethy held that 'life did not depend on the organization of the body' but existed as a material substance 'superadded' to the body; something akin to electricity.[10] Influenced by the French materialists, Lawrence argued that there could be no 'vital force' separate from the body. He gave lectures and published papers explaining his views, stating his scepticism and ridiculing Abernethy's standpoint as old-fashioned. Abernethy was religious whereas Lawrence wanted to distance medicine from religion and he later had connections with radical journalists. It was not until 1822, the year Shelley died, that Lawrence made an official recantation for the sake of his career.[11] Lawrence's views influenced Shelley as early as June 1811. He was to develop them in writings such as *A Refutation of Deism*, *On Life* and *On a Future State* and to use the imagery and ideas of the debate in works including *A Defence of Poetry* and *Prometheus Unbound*.[12] He also used what medical knowledge he had gained to treat friends and family.[13]

Although Timothy had agreed with John Grove that Shelley should have an allowance of £200, he did not pay it. He was attempting to use economic means to force his son to recant his views, but this Shelley never did. He now made some decisions and connections which were to lead to cutting himself off completely from his class and attempting to live his life as far as possible in accordance with the principles of *Political Justice*, *Rights of Man* and other progressive ideals. *Political Justice* argues clearly that aristocracy, the church and property laws, including marriage, are barriers to achieving an equal society: 'aristocracy like monarchy is founded in falshood'.[14] In *Rights of Man*, Paine states that the aristocratic class is unfit to govern since 'in a family of six children, five are exposed. Aristocracy has never more than one child'.[15] He is referring to the system of primogeniture in which the eldest son inherits the property to the exclusion of the younger children, comparing it to ancient Sparta where unwanted female babies were left to die. In language closely echoing Paine's, Shelley said: 'The aristocracy condemn all but their first-born to starvation, and place in his hands the rod of despotism [. . .] I am one of these aristocrats. [. . .] My first, act, when in possession of my estate, shall be to divide it equally with my family.'[16]

Accordingly, he wrote to his father's solicitor:

As common report, & tolerably good authority informs me that part of Sir Bysshe Shelley's property is entailed upon me; I am willing by signature to resign all pretensions to such property, in case my father will divide it equally with my sisters & my mother & allow me now 100£ per an[num] as an annuity which will only amount to 2000£, perhaps less.[17]

Whitton refused, saying he was 'not a willing instrument by which insult may be offered to your father' and passed the letter to Timothy, who said he had 'never felt such a shock in my life, infinitely more than when I heard of his expulsion'.[18] From then on the correspondence between Shelley and Whitton was hostile and arrogant on both sides. Whitton kept up the feud between father and son by reporting everything he heard about Shelley in an unfavourable light, writing remarks such as, 'I had from P.B. Shelley the most scurrilous letter that a mad viper could dictate'.[19] Shelley was from a legal point of view, wrong, and Timothy must have known that it was not easy to break an entail but his rage stemmed from his son's attitude which threatened not just the Shelley family and their position but the whole class and system. Although Timothy was later to describe him as 'such a Pupil of Godwin', Shelley had been able to observe the social and financial situation of his sisters and was aware that Elizabeth was already having to consider marriage.[20]

Shelley believed that 'equality is natural' and that 'political virtue' should 'approximate to this ideal point of perfection'. It is not surprising that he next formed what his father considered, as other members of his class would have, a *mésalliance*, although it was not with 'a Servant, or some person of very low birth', as the Earl of Chichester thought. Chichester certainly knew Timothy who may have given him this impression.[21] Shelley's sisters were at school in Clapham, where he went to see them. In January 1811, his 14-year-old sister Mary, probably hoping to help him get over his grief over Harriet Grove by this introduction, gave him a present to deliver to a 16-year-old schoolfellow, Harriet Westbrook, 'a very handsome girl' with 'hair like a poet's dream'. Shelley visited her with Charles Grove before returning to Oxford.[22]

Harriet's father was wealthy enough to live in the fashionable Grosvenor Square area of London. He had made his money from taverns and coffee houses and owned a coffee house in neighbouring Mount Street which seems to have been a favourite Whig rendezvous – Hogg believed it 'infested with Irish patriots'.[23] If so, Harriet's elder sister, Eliza, then about 28, may have been well-informed about politics from discussions with her father and his friends; Mr Westbrook asked Shelley to join them one evening. Shelley described the sisters as 'both very clever, & the youngest (*my* friend) is amiable' but he at first had reservations about Eliza, remarking that she was 'too civil by half'.[24] He realised that the sisters, as daughters of a tavern-keeper, would not normally have the entrée to the society of heirs to landed estates and might regard him as a 'catch'. Eliza herself thought that his family might break up any relationship with them and asked him not to give 'any notice to your sister Mary, or indeed any of your family, of your intimacy with us'.[25] Before the year was out the tavern-keeper's daughters had been received into the home of the premier Duke of England, the Duke of Norfolk.

During this time, Shelley developed his political connections by meeting Leigh Hunt for breakfast and having dinner with Norfolk. Charles Grove said that Norfolk attempted 'to shackle [Shelley's] mind' with 'a plan for bringing him in as member for Horsham [. . .] and introduc[ing] him into life as a mere follower of the Duke',[26] but, since an atheist could not enter Parliament, it was out of the question for Shelley. Norfolk may have hinted that a candidate could subscribe officially to the Church of England while keeping his own beliefs quiet, as he himself probably did, but Shelley's public rejection of religion would have required an equally public recantation which Norfolk would have realised was not possible. Perhaps this discussion took place earlier. Their relationship remained sufficiently cordial for Shelley to ask Norfolk to intervene with his family later.[27]

Radical Politics

Shelley started to become active in radical politics. He and Charles Grove attended the British Forum where political debates were held. Grove's description makes light of Shelley's visit and his part in the debate there, saying:

> It was then a spouting club in which Gale Jones and other Radicals abused all existing governments. Bysshe made so good a speech, complimenting and differing from the previous orators, that when he left the room there was a rush to find out who he was, and to induce him to attend there again. He gave them a false name and address, not caring a farthing about the meeting, or the subjects here discussed.[28]

It is very unlikely that Shelley would have been so indifferent to the subjects or to the members of the British Forum who wished him to return. In 1810, Charles Philip Yorke (Home Secretary 1802–04) had insisted that the public was excluded from the House of Commons debate over the 'Walcheren disaster'. The British Forum debated this decision and condemned it, and John Gale Jones, formerly a surgeon and member of the London Corresponding Society, printed an announcement of this and placed it outside the House of Commons.[29] Jones was sent to Newgate and was still there in April 1811. Burdett moved that Jones should be discharged, and published a letter in Cobbett's *Political Register* denying the power of the House of Commons to imprison. As a result of this Burdett himself was committed to the Tower after a sensational arrest and much popular support. Jones was eventually freed in June but was re-arrested and sent back to Newgate, this time for 'libelling' Lord Castlereagh. As this was so closely linked to what had happened to Finnerty, it is probable that Shelley would have gone to the British Forum to hear other debates, especially since it was located in Poland Street, where Shelley and Hogg had taken a room on their arrival in London.[30]

In 1811, Britain was still at war with France and the national debt had increased hugely. The issue of paper money had caused inflation. The notes were easily forged and it was difficult for people to tell the difference between fake and genuine. There were many hangings for forgery and banks failed.[31] More money was spent on the 2,000 prosecutions and 300 executions between 1797 and 1821 than was lost through forgery.[32] There was great public anger about this. Meanwhile, the government expenditure on the Royal Family was excessive – in 1817 the *extra* money voted for the king and Prince Regent was £500,000 and £20,000 of that went on snuffboxes! Yet when the cotton workers had presented a petition to the Prince Regent early in 1811 it was ignored. The royal family was most unpopular, but stockbrokers and bankers were a close second.[33]

George III was ill with porphyria, diagnosed then as madness, and a relapse in November 1810 had enabled his son, later George IV, to become Prince Regent. When younger, the prince had been close to Fox, Sheridan and Norfolk, but as Prince Regent he rejected all their principles and behaved in a completely self-indulgent way. In June he gave a lavish fête for 2,000 guests at Carlton House, installing an artificial stream. Grove says that Shelley wrote a poem which 'he published immediately' in mid-June 1811 and threw copies of it into the 'carriages of persons going to Carlton House'.[34] The Groves had been invited to attend and Shelley, then back home at Field Place, came to London. Grove's account sounds as if he were an eyewitness and a letter to Edward Fergus Graham, who had taught the Shelleys music, suggests that he was also present.[35]

" King Pyrrhus cur'd his splenetic
And testy courtiers with a kick." .....
Hudibras.

Figure 3 'The Figure' (the Prince Regent), from *The Queen that Jack Found* (London: John Fairburn, 1820). (Photograph by William Alderson, kind permission of Nora Crook)

Shelley wrote to another friend commenting on 'the bubbling *brooks & mossy banks* at Carlton House'. 'Here are a people advanced [. . .] wilfully rushing to a revolution, the natural death of all great commercial empires, which must plunge them in the barbarism from which they are slowly arising.' He saw that the Regent's extravagance was making him ludicrous and detested and he expected a revolution. He was not in favour of 'popular insurrections and revolutions' but said 'if *such things must be* I will take the side of the People'.[36]

Shelley returned to Sussex with his views strengthened and went to stay initially with his uncle, Captain John Pilfold, in Cuckfield. Pilfold managed successfully to get Timothy to restore his son's allowance which Timothy had revoked almost immediately after he had agreed it with John Grove. Shelley was also granted 'freedom of action', although when he went back to Field Place he had to act secretively as Timothy did not want him at home, believing that his opinions would influence Elizabeth. While Timothy was away, Shelley finally invited Hogg to Horsham. Hogg was enamoured of Elizabeth but Shelley now discouraged him, probably because Elizabeth was not interested.[37] This was the beginning of a pattern in the relationship between Hogg, Shelley and women connected to Shelley which has been taken as evidence of a latent homoerotic relationship between them. Shortly after Shelley's return home, an anonymous letter arrived accusing Shelley's mother of an affair with Edward Graham, the music master. 'We all laughed heartily,' Shelley told Graham, '& thought it a good opportunity of making up. But he is as inveterate as ever'.[38]

At his uncle's, Shelley became acquainted with Elizabeth Hitchener, a schoolteacher about ten years older than he was, with whom he began an intense correspondence, discussing with her ideas on the traditional landed aristocracy and the new 'aristocracy' based on wealth made on the Stock Exchange. He would develop these ideas in *A Philosophical View of Reform*. While 'purse-proud ignorance & illiterateness' was 'more contemptible' than aristocracy, he believed that 'all monopolies are bad [. . .] a state of equality (if attainable) were preferable to any other'. He denounced a luxurious way of living, 'mahogany tables, silver vases'.[39] It is clear from his 1817 essay *On The*

Game Laws how much he despised the traditional aristocracy and the way in which they manipulated the law in their favour.

His rank in society was a barrier to communicating with those of a lower class. Eliza Westbrook had hinted at it, Hitchener was reluctant to pursue a correspondence with him because of it and, while staying with his cousin, Thomas Grove, at his estate in Wales, he met a beggar who said, 'I see by your dress that you are a rich man – they have injured me & mine a million times. You appear to be well intentioned but I have no security of it while you live in such a house as that, or wear such clothes as those'. Shelley was never to live in such a house as that again and during the rest of his life he wore simple clothes 'of cotton jean'.[40] He no longer saw himself as an aristocrat and was building up a circle of people with whom he felt he had political and religious ideas in common, probably considering living with them as a nucleus of a free-thinking society: Hogg, Hitchener, the Westbrooks.

Marriage

Shelley was staying with the Groves before going on to Aberystwyth where Mr. Westbrook had a house, and from there he planned to go on to York to see Hogg. This roundabout journey was in order to conceal the two later visits from his father, who had discovered Hogg's visit to Horsham. While with the Groves, his plans changed. He found out that Harriet Westbrook was to go back after the summer to the Clapham school where she was being bullied because she corresponded with him. Shelley went back to London, via Horsham where he borrowed some money from T.C. Medwin, and with Charles Grove's help he eloped with Harriet to Scotland to be married.[41]

Shelley had told Hogg in May to 'read the marriage service before you *think* of allowing an amiable beloved female to submit to such degradation' but by August he said that Hogg's arguments for marriage had made him 'a perfect convert' since a relationship without marriage in 1811 caused a woman a 'disproportionate sacrifice'. He was to say later that he was 'inclined to think the Godwinian plan is best' but at present he understood that 'a previous reformation in morals, and that a general & a great one is requisite before it [marriage] may be remedied'.[42] The 'Godwinian plan' suggests that the relationship between a man and a woman should be like 'any other species of friendship' with 'the unforced consent of either party' and to 'engross one woman to myself' was 'the most odious of all monopolies'.[43] This sounds very male-centred but both Godwin and Shelley respected the views of the women they knew. There were unmarried couples who lived together under a fiction that they were legally married and independent women who worked and brought up their illegitimate children as Charlotte Dacre did.[44] So did Mary Jane, Godwin's second wife, whose older children, Charles and Claire Clairmont, were illegitimate. Claire's father was a member of the Somerset landed gentry.[45]

Shelley probably discussed his ideas against marriage with the Westbrooks. He had given Harriet his book, *St. Irvyne*, in which marriage is referred to as 'but a chain'. Harriet had presented him, in turn, with Amelia Opie's *Adeline Mowbray*, which purports to show that a free love relationship cannot succeed even with the highest ideals because of the prejudices of society. This was based on the life of Mary Wollstonecraft. She had lived first with Gilbert Imlay and had a daughter, Fanny, and then with Godwin whom she married when pregnant with their daughter, Mary, who was to become Shelley's second wife. After Wollstonecraft's death in childbirth in 1797, Godwin wrote about her life in an honest way, but it brought her general condemnation. Shelley may have first read Wollstonecraft's works in 1812 and he admired her deeply.[46]

Harriet Westbrook was no Wollstonecraft, but her letters reveal a charming personality. She seems straightforward, friendly, intelligent, with some political commitment and certainly great sympathy for the poor and oppressed. Shelley himself described her as 'a really noble soul'. His often-repeated explanation that he married Harriet because she was distraught at the idea of going back to school appears to be true as far as it goes, but he was also extremely attracted to her: Hellen Shelley said that Harriet was his 'particular admiration'.[47] He thought of her as 'one of the crushers' (a reference to Voltaire's *Ecrasez l'Infame*, 'Crush Superstition'), but he did not intend to give up his other 'crushers', initially planning to live with Hogg as well as Harriet, and he asked Hitchener to live with them shortly afterwards.[48] Hogg joined the Shelleys in Edinburgh after they were married and they returned to York together.

Timothy stopped Shelley's allowance on hearing of the marriage, so he and Harriet were penniless. After writing repeated letters to his father without getting any agreement about the allowance and becoming more and more angry, Shelley returned to Sussex. On a visit to Field Place he was in such rage that, according to Timothy, his mother and sister were so frightened that they would run upstairs 'if they heard a Dog Bark'. Timothy added that Shelley had 'nothing to say but the £200'. Clearly, he realised the cause of his son's anger and, although he took the moral high ground, Timothy was also inclined to be 'irate'.[49] Shelley then wrote a letter to his mother accusing her of encouraging a plan for Graham to marry Elizabeth in order to conceal her own affair with him. This idea was based on the anonymous letter they had all laughed at in the spring and was, as his father said, 'too absurd and ridiculous'.[50] Shelley's violent, uncontrollable rages caused him to make unfounded accusations.

Returning to York, Shelley found that Eliza Westbrook had preceded him. She had brought much-needed money, but there was a more serious reason for her presence. While Shelley was away, Hogg had been making unwelcome sexual advances to Harriet. Shelley decided to break with Hogg, which was hard for them both, and move to Keswick in the Lake District. Shelley showed some maturity in his letters to Hogg, explaining that he did not believe that any sexual relationship should be forced, he was afraid Hogg would force it, and he had put Harriet's wishes first.[51] This was not to renounce his commitment to free love, it was to protect Harriet. Hogg had only superficial feelings for Harriet – he not long before had been madly in love with Elizabeth. Shelley's group of 'crushers' now consisted of himself, Harriet and Eliza.

Shelley had developed both politically and psychologically between the end of March when he was expelled from Oxford and the beginning of November when he left for the Lakes, a period of just over six months in which he turned 19. He had stood firm against the pressure to repudiate or conceal his opinions about religion. With a parliamentary career now closed to him, he was following more radical politics and had spoken successfully at the British Forum. He had made two contacts who were eminent in their respective fields and who were to become close friends within a couple of years: Leigh Hunt and Lawrence. He was attempting to live as close as he could to his political ideals. Although he did not want a 'monopolistic' marriage but to live in a group with like-minded people, he married Harriet to protect her from disrespect. He had not continued with his medical studies but he could not afford them and he may have realised that it would be difficult to combine a dedication to medicine with a life in literature and politics.

From a psychological point of view he had survived the expulsion from Oxford with the ruin of his education and career and his father's lack of understanding and rigid opposition which had left him with no money more than once. Incidentally, he had paid his printing costs from the allowance he had received in June.[52] He had coped with Hogg's obsessions first with his sister and then with his wife, but had now broken with his closest friend as well as with his family. These stressful circumstances had taken their toll. Tom Medwin mentioned a return of the sleepwalking after the expulsion. Shelley had exhibited violent rages towards his family and Whitton. He spoke of 'nervous' illnesses for which he had taken laudanum, confirmed by Harriet's remark to Hitchener that she hoped he would 'outgrow his nervous complaints'.[53] These may have taken the form described by Leigh Hunt's son, Thornton, of 'suddenly throwing up his book and hands, sliding off his chair, pouring forth loud and continuous shrieks, "stamping his feet madly on the ground"'.[54] These fits seem to be conditions brought on by stress, but not the insanity suggested by his father and others.

Lake District

Shelley, Harriet and Eliza lived at Keswick from November 1811 to early February 1812. In December they visited Norfolk at his nearby home, Greystoke. Norfolk intervened with Shelley's father, who restored his allowance. Harriet's father allowed her the same amount, but they were never to live within their means.[55] As three children of very wealthy people, they had never learnt to budget. All would take for granted a degree of comfort which less well-off people would not

Figure 4 An engraving by G.J. Stodart of the portrait of Shelley aged about twelve, by the Duc de Montpensier. (Photograph by William Alderson, kind permission of Nora Crook)

expect and they were used to getting what they wanted and someone else paying the bill. Shelley grossly underestimated what he needed to live on. Although he himself dressed and ate simply, he needed books and, as well as wanting to get his own writing published, he wanted to help others do so. He took seriously the idea that it was his duty to help less well-off people than himself and he did it with money he did not yet possess. Bills, left unpaid, accrued interest so became even more impossible to pay.[56]

Shelley had hoped to meet Robert Southey, William Wordsworth and Samuel Coleridge, the poets from the previous generation whose poetry and political ideas, influenced by the French Revolution, had inspired him. He met only Southey, who was kind and helpful to him, conversed with him, allowed him to use his library and helped get the rent on the cottage reduced.[57] Shelley initially regarded Southey as a 'great Man' but decided that 'his mind [was] terribly narrow' when he realised that Southey had not only changed his opinions but also enthusiastically hoped he could convert Shelley, who reminded him of his own youthful self.[58] Southey told Shelley that he believed in revolution, egalitarianism and liberty, but 'not in this age' and that when Shelley was older he would think the same.

To this effect, Southey may have discussed the French Revolution with Shelley. Southey was to publish, in the June 1812 *Quarterly Review*, a review of *Biographie Moderne* (1811), a biographical dictionary which included 'the French Revolutionists'. Southey's purpose was to show that they were not to be admired. He regarded Babeuf's ideas as the most dangerous, but he misrepresented them by quoting not from him but from Sylvain Maréchal's *Manifesto of the Equals*, a document Babeuf disagreed with.[59] In 1797, however, Southey had said that if Babeuf had been put to death there was 'no man left whom we may compare with the Grecians'. In 1802, he told Coleridge that Babeuf was 'a great man' adding that Mary Wollstonecraft had told him Babeuf was 'the most extraordinary one she had ever seen' and that his 'system of total equalization would have been wise [. . .] and would have rendered any return to common systems impossible & excited insurrection all over Europe' but Babeuf 'did not set sail till the tide had set in against him'.[60] Shelley shared Southey's great admiration for Wollstonecraft. It is possible that Southey may have shown him the review and shared his earlier views of Babeuf and those of Wollstonecraft, but in any case Shelley had the opportunity of seeing it when it was published. Southey did not support Shelley's plans to go to Ireland. He was virulently anti-Catholic and opposed to Catholic Emancipation. Shelley told Hitchener that he passed

Southey's house on leaving Keswick without a pang, but Southey knew Godwin and gave Shelley his address, so Shelley wrote to him.[61]

The Lake District was not entirely wild and rural. There was a copper mine at Keswick and small factories, probably for wool or cotton products as in neighbouring Westmorland.[62] Since their hours were so long, it would have been difficult for Shelley to have gained knowledge of the conditions of factory workers through talking to them, but he did talk to working people whenever he had the opportunity. To Hitchener, he wrote, 'I have beheld scenes of misery. The manufacture[r]s [factory workers] are reduced to starvation.'[63] Shelley greatly appreciated the beautiful mountain scenery, but his attitude towards the factories was not purely an 'aesthetic' reaction, nor was he alone in his view. The workers themselves dreaded factories and mills as centres of exploitation, cruelty and immorality and child prisons where children worked twelve hours a day, going to sleep at their machines, and were locked up to prevent their running away.[64] They were beginning to organise: spinners in the Manchester area had struck in 1810.

In 1799, the Government had passed the Combination Acts which banned unions although, where employers needed workers, this legislation was not always heeded. There were some successful unions among the London shoemakers and tailors, but in 1810 the compositors on *The Times* were prosecuted for combining and other unions met in secret.[65] Theoretically, the laws prevented employers from 'combining' too, but they were always used against working people. Weavers, like shoemakers or hatters, tended to be relatively prosperous self-employed artisans, working in small workshops. Their incomes were falling, so they petitioned the government only to find that it no longer acted for employees. They sank more and more into poverty and despair, and by 1811 a weaver was earning less than a poorly paid agricultural labourer. Agricultural labourers were also losing their work to mechanisation, and whereas traditionally they had lived at the farmhouse, they now had the expense of food and housing. Many could not survive and sought poor relief.[66]

Framework knitters, who made stockings on a narrow frame, were self-employed specialised craftsmen. They petitioned Parliament for regulation of the industry because hosiers were ruining their trade by getting material knitted on a large frame and cutting it up into cheaper, poorer-quality shapes. The committees promised to look into it but had made arrests for sedition or for illegal union activity. In Nottingham, bands called 'Luddites', after Ned Ludd, a probably fictitious leader, broke into hosiers' shops and smashed the frames, supported by the local population. By November 1811, 2,000 troops were there.[67] Shelley remarked, 'Curses light on them for their motives if they destroy one of its famine-wasted inhabitants.'[68] Machines also threatened the livelihood of the highly skilled croppers (cloth finishers). Machine breaking and food riots spread to Yorkshire, Cheshire and Lancashire, where £100,000 worth of property was destroyed. 121,000 troops were stationed between Leicester and York, more than in Spain. Employers felt they had a right to shoot at anyone attacking their shops. Luddites were killed or left to die, but when a Leeds employer was killed, Parliament passed a Framebreaking Bill (February 1812) making framebreaking a capital offence.[69]

The bill was too late to hang those arrested at Nottingham and the success of the Nottinghamshire Luddites led them to organise a national union. It was broken within the year by a 'combination' of employers; their association was also illegal under the 1799 Combination Acts, but they were not prosecuted. When framebreakers were hanged in Lancashire, Cheshire and York in 1813, Shelley, Harriet and Eliza subscribed to a fund for the relief of their families.[70]

Ireland and Catholic Emancipation

Shelley wanted to form a political organisation such as he had described to Leigh Hunt the previous year, but, as he could not do this on his own, he needed to build it within an existing movement. Such a movement was developing in Ireland.

In the eighteenth century, the Protestant Ascendancy appeared self-confident in their wealth and power but they were a small minority and there was much resentment. Catholics had been dispossessed, while Dissenters felt they deserved a better deal for supporting the British. The Penal Laws prohibited Catholics from inheriting or buying land from Protestants, and by the mid-century only 5 per cent of land in Ireland belonged to Catholics. Non-Anglicans were also obliged to pay tithes to the established church and were barred by religious tests from university, the armed services, municipal employment and the law. Since, if they went to school they were required to become Protestant, many Catholics were taught illegally by 'hedge schoolmasters'. Rural secret societies, such as the Whiteboys, were formed to fight against enclosures or tithes.[71]

The Irish lived in extreme poverty, exacerbated by their English landlords living in England rather than on their extensive estates in Ireland. Many emigrated to England or America or joined the French or Austrian armies.[72] But with perceived growing prosperity through a strong textile industry there was greater resentment of Poyning's Law which required the bills of the Irish Parliament to be approved by the English privy council. During the American War of Independence, groups of Volunteers were formed to defend Ireland against possible invasion by France and Spain. Although Catholics were officially not allowed to bear arms, many Catholics joined the Volunteers. The Volunteers' strength obtained the removal of some penal laws, the repeal of Poyning's Law and the independence of the Bank of Ireland. In 1793, Catholics who had freehold property of 40 shillings (£2.00) were granted the vote and were allowed to enter professions such as law. Subsequently Maynooth College was established so that priests could be educated in Ireland.[73]

The Catholic Committee had been formed to campaign for Catholic Emancipation but was dominated by aristocrats. In 1790, new committee members, who later became prominent United Irishmen, encouraged all Catholics of whatever class to sign a petition demanding relief from the penal laws. The aristocratic leaders of the Catholic Committee refused to support them and seceded in December 1791. Protestant liberals in Ulster formed the United Irishmen to gain equal representation and an independent Ireland and campaigned for Catholic Emancipation.[74] Catholics increasingly joined them and the movement spread all over the country, in some cases incorporating the Catholic Defenders, originally a society along the lines of the Whiteboys. The United Irishmen were internationalists with links in England, Scotland and France (they had sent representatives to the 1792 Scottish Convention). They supported traditional Irish culture and in 1792 the Belfast Festival featured the

great harpists still living.[75] They commissioned a cheap edition of
Paine's *Rights of Man* in 1791 and distributed 'huge quantities' free
of charge, newspapers published extracts and 40,000 copies were
sold.[76] A song of the same title was made.[77] In June 1797, between
Belfast and Dublin 'almost everyone [was] an open well-wisher to
the United Irishmen', but the United Irishmen were outlawed in 1794
and so became a secret society.[78]

After the failure of the 1797 French expedition, another was
planned for 1798, but in March many of the United Irish leaders
were arrested in Dublin, betrayed by an informer. The army began to
raid villages and towns looking for arms. They searched and burned
cottages, set up triangles in the town squares and flogged people until
they gave up their pikes. Some had none to give up. The remaining
United Irish leaders went ahead with the rising in Dublin but it failed
(once again because of informers) and the leaders were arrested.
There was confusion and in some country towns people attempted a
rising, in others they did not.[79] Although there were brave attempts
in other places, such as County Antrim and County Down, Wexford
was where the rebels held out for longest. They set up a republic with
green boughs and notices for 'LIBERTY and EQUALITY', but after
three weeks the army arrived and the leaders were executed.[80]

The French who landed were captured by the British and the rising
failed but it was clear to Pitt that the bigoted and arrogant Protestant
Ascendancy was incapable of governing Ireland.[81] Rather than allow
reforms, Pitt pushed through the 1801 Act of Union by creating
peerages. The rich left for England, taking their custom with them so
artisans lost their livelihood, the Belfast linen industry suffered and
the poor sank into even deeper poverty. Pitt had intended to introduce
Catholic Emancipation but the king was against it. Pitt resigned,
although he became Prime Minister again when war resumed with
France in 1803. That year Robert Emmet led a rebellion which failed,
but his name was to inspire Irishmen – and Shelley.[82]

In Ireland, the Catholic Committee had not only revived but
was winning victories. In November 1810, Peter Finnerty had
recommended a Petition to Parliament for Catholic Emancipation
and for the repeal of the Union, supported by a successful lawyer,
Daniel O'Connell. Protestants supported these demands because of

the poverty and loss of trade caused by the Union.[83] Although the 1793 Convention Act forbade the meeting of delegates, in October 1811 the Catholic Committee managed to meet, draft a petition and disperse before the police arrived. Six delegates were arrested, but when the first came to trial he was acquitted to a 'deafening peal of triumph [. . .] waving of hats and clapping of hands: the news ran like wildfire through the streets'.[84] To evade the law against 'delegates', the committee threw their meetings open; O'Connell stood on the bridge which now bears his name inviting all and sundry.[85] A strong political movement such as this would be likely to have some among it who would see beyond immediate aims to equality and internationalism.

Campaigning in Ireland

Shelley, who would have known of the 1810 meeting through the Finnerty campaign, said that he considered Ireland as 'constituting a part of a great crisis in opinions'. He first spoke of the decision to go to Ireland shortly after his return from his visit to Greystoke where no doubt he had discussed the situation with Norfolk. He felt confident enough to ask Norfolk for £100 towards the trip, which he didn't get, and to begin his *Address to the Irish People*, the title referring to Wolfe Tone's 1796 *Address to the People of Ireland*.[86] It drew on Paine's work, so popular in Ireland. At the beginning of February 1812, Shelley, Eliza and Harriet left for Ireland where Shelley had the *Address* printed by Stockdale, printer of the *Press*. Shelley undoubtedly chose him for his political connections, but Stockdale had turned informer.[87]

Shelley's actions in Ireland contradict claims that he was afraid of a 'mob' or of working people.[88] He told Godwin that the *Address* was 'principally designed to operate on the Irish *mob*'.[89] He immediately recruited Daniel Healy to distribute it in pubs and paste it on walls, therefore encouraging contact with working people who came to call on him. Healy left with a pile every day, 1,500 were circulated and 'excited a sensation of wonder', 'made a stir' and 'set some men's minds afloat'. Shelley and Harriet handed copies out in the street and threw them off the balcony of the house where they stayed.[90] Shelley befriended members of 'the mob', spending what money he had in relieving poverty. He tried to prevent an orphan from being conscripted into the army and he was attempting to help an Irishman, Redfern, who had been press-ganged into the British Army in Portugal, by taking the case up with Burdett. Shelley succeeded in preventing a widow woman being arrested for stealing a loaf although the constable told him 'he was called out to business of this nature sometimes 20 times in a night'. Shelley said, 'The rich grind the poor into abjectness, and then complain that they are abject. They goad them to famine, and hang them if they steal a loaf'.[91] Eliza was collecting extracts from Paine for publication. Shelley remarked, 'in one thing at least none of us are deficient, viz. zeal and sincerity. – '[92]

Both the *Address* and the *Proposals for an Association of Philanthropists*, Shelley's next Irish pamphlet, support Catholic Emancipation and the Repeal of the Union.[93] The *Address* looks beyond these to a distribution of wealth (p. 26). Shelley opposes the divide between rich and poor, saying that it was 'horrible that the lower classes must waste their lives and liberty to furnish means for their oppressors [...] Nature never intended that there should be such a thing as a poor man or a rich one'. Irishmen should reform themselves and improve their minds (p. 29) in readiness for a time 'when no Government will be wanted but that of your neighbour's opinion' (pp. 31, 24, 25). He agrees with Quakers on non-violence and is against war (pp. 17, 30), urges open meetings rather than secret societies (p. 18), warns against trusting the Regent (p. 20) and says that it is the ruling class which is against Ireland, not 'the sense of the country' (p. 21). He has been criticised for his patronising tone, although there were similar pamphlets in circulation. But, in the hope of countering religious prejudice and with an eventual aim of countering religion, Shelley attacked the Catholic religion before he did the Protestant and so was likely to lose Catholic readers immediately since those who are oppressed for their religion are more likely to defend it than to admit flaws they privately see themselves. Shelley told Hitchener he wanted to 'to induce Quakerish and Socinian principle[s] of politics'.[94] Communities of Quakers, however, had been established in Ireland since the late seventeenth century and were much respected, particularly for their activities in 1798 so it is difficult to see how Shelley could have done more than they did themselves by example.

Shelley's *Proposals*, which he had printed in Dublin, mentioned Godwin and Paine (p. 52) and were intended to appeal to a more politically aware group of people than the *Address*. Shelley said that he sought to set up an Association, open rather than secret, to work towards an egalitarian republic and support equality of law and freedom of the press. He recognised that this Association 'would be obnoxious to the government' as well as to 'aristocracy' and 'priesthood' but stated 'the present state of politics and morals is wrong' (p. 44). Although it is worth working for Catholic Emancipation as a progressive aim, it will not benefit poorer Catholics and so the Repeal of the Union is more important (pp. 42–4). The pamphlet shows a softening towards Jesus for his egalitarian teaching, though not towards the religion which does not follow his precepts (p. 46). Shelley also printed a *Declaration of Rights* in Dublin, drawing these largely from the 1789 and 1793 French constitutions. They open with a statement included in the *Proposals*: 'Government has no rights, it is a delegation for the purpose of securing them for others'.

Shelley had hoped to build on the memory of the United Irishmen, but most of those who were not executed or transported after 1798 had fled abroad or changed their opinions, like Hamilton Rowan and Curran, whose addresses Godwin had given Shelley. Although Curran, now Master of the Rolls which Shelley '[did] not like him for', had refused to sign an order for the arrest of the delegates to the Catholic Committee, he had also refused the brief to defend Robert Emmet and disowned his daughter, Sarah, for her attachment to him.[95] Although Shelley said he had 'met with no determined Republicans',[96] the *Address* had attracted not only Healy, who was said to be willing to 'go through fire and water' for him, but John Lawless, a supporter of the Catholic Committee with United Irishmen connections, and Catherine Nugent, a former active member of the United Irishmen who worked at a furrier's as seamstress. Shelley planned to set up a newspaper and 'a debating society' with Lawless and to collaborate with him on his *Compendium of the History of Ireland* (1814). Later, he wished to publish William McNevin's *Pieces of Irish History*, but he could not raise the money for these projects.[97]

It is not improbable that O'Connell would have welcomed Shelley as a fellow campaigner despite Shelley's Republican views since

William Thompson, known as a Red Republican, campaigned for Catholic Emancipation in 1812.[98] Although he was to die a devout Catholic, O'Connell, while studying in London in the 1790s, had read Godwin and Paine avidly, and had then considered himself a Deist. O'Connell sometimes said that he would give up Catholic Emancipation if the Union were repealed.[99] This is less startling than it sounds since an Irish Parliament would be under pressure to grant emancipation. Shelley was able to speak at the 28 February meeting at the Fishamble Street Theatre where he supported the aims of the Committee, blaming the Union for the poverty he saw in Ireland and calling for religious freedom. The audience 'hissed [him] when he spoke of religion' but they liked his political comments. He tactfully refrained from attacking the Prince for reneging on Catholic Emancipation since O'Connell had not yet done so. There were favourable reports in the Dublin papers, one probably written by Lawless who contributed to the *Weekly Messenger*, and a hostile letter signed 'An Englishman'.[100]

Shelley did not see that he had done well in attracting supporters and speaking at the Catholic Committee meeting. He came to think of his period in Ireland as a failure because in the face of such poverty he was unable to rapidly recruit to the Association. Probably Godwin's attitude contributed to this as, even though Shelley advocated peaceful meetings, Godwin accused him of 'preparing a scene of blood'. Nevertheless, Shelley argued strongly against Godwin's disapproval and realised that he had to go beyond Godwin, and beyond Paine.[101] In order to build on these successes, however, he would have had to remain in Ireland which he had not planned to do. Later, O'Connell's son, John, thought that Shelley's warning that the 'higher orders' of Catholics would be the ones to benefit from Catholic Emancipation had proved only too true. Although Daniel O'Connell effected small reforms when he was elected to the British Parliament, his pleas to that Parliament, as a broken-hearted, dying man, for help for the starving Irish people in the Great Famines of the 1840s were powerless.[102]

O'Connell's movement and the reform movement in England were organised on the system Shelley suggested, but building a successful single-issue mass movement is not at all the same as Shelley's plan to set up Associations and '*quietly* revolutionise the country'.[103] For this, Shelley would have needed to work within the mass movements to attract the most politically aware. He was not sufficiently discouraged as to have no hopes of building an Association in England, however, and he sent copies of his *Declaration of Rights* to Hitchener. Spies at the Catholic Committee meeting had mentioned Shelley in their reports. His parcel to Hitchener was opened, and its contents sent to the Secretary of State. Hitchener was 'watched' by government spies and a report by Lord Chichester was sent to the Home Office.[104]

Devon and Wales

Shelley, Eliza, Harriet and Healy left Ireland in March 1812 and travelled through Wales, stopping at Thomas Grove's. Shelley thought of taking a nearby farm, Nangtwillt, which he may have hoped would be a communal farm as he invited both Hitchener and Nugent to come and live there, but he was 19, a minor, and could not raise any money for the lease. They travelled on to Lynmouth, a fishing village near Barnstaple, Devon, where they settled in modest lodgings, shared with others, and made friends with Mrs Hooper, their landlady.[105]

England in 1812 was in an economic crisis. Bonaparte's attempt to seize British goods and trade embargo against Britain (the 'Continental System') led to the British Orders in Council forbidding trade with France and its possessions. Trade with Europe slumped. Britain's seizing and searching American ships was to cause another unpopular war. The price of bread rose and there were food riots in Bristol, Manchester and other areas including Barnstaple. There were riots over enclosures in the Lleyn Peninsula near Tremadog in Wales. In Cornwall, the tin miners struck and marched to Truro, the county town. The Luddite risings also continued. In May, the Prime Minister, Spencer Perceval, was shot dead – to evident jubilation, the assassin a popular hero.[106]

In 1811 the elderly but still active Cartwright had begun to form clubs to campaign for reform and toured the country, including Luddite areas, getting 200,000 signatures on petitions. The clubs were named after John Hampden, the MP who had started the campaign to oppose Charles I's ship money tax and who was one of those whose attempted arrest sparked the Civil War in 1642. Burdett was a member. The weavers, whose appeals to Parliament were ignored, began to take up the cause of reform.[107] The Prince Regent was unpopular for reneging on his commitment to Catholic Emancipation, and when the *Morning Post*, a royalist newspaper, celebrated his 1812 birthday with a panegyric describing him, among other things, as an 'Adonis of Loveliness', *The Examiner* responded that he was 'a corpulent man of fifty, a violator of his word, a libertine over head and ears in debt and disgrace'. Although this was true, the editors, John and Leigh Hunt, were subsequently sentenced to two years in prison for saying so.[108] An elderly radical, Daniel Isaac Eaton, had already suffered seven prosecutions and 15 months of imprisonment. Juries had acquitted him three times. He was now condemned to the pillory for publishing Paine's *Age of Reason*, but 'the mob' cheered him and offered him glasses of wine and biscuits, flags and flowers in the pillory.[109]

Shelley shared the indignation of 'the mob'. He wrote *A Letter to Lord Ellenborough*, the judge who had convicted Eaton, and had it printed in Barnstaple. The *Letter* implies that the prosecutor had stirred up the jury, as Christians, against Eaton as a Deist and criticises Ellenborough for not intervening to point out the irrelevancy of this to the case. Shelley asks what crime Eaton had committed, whom he had injured and what right had Ellenborough to prosecute him for his beliefs. He points out, as he did in *The Necessity of Atheism*, that a belief cannot be compelled. 'The time is rapidly approaching [. . .] when the Mahometan, the Jew, the Christian, the Deist, and the Atheist will live together in one community [. . .] united in the bonds of charity and brotherly love'. He is horrified that such prosecutions continue in 'a nation that presumptuously calls itself the sanctuary of freedom'.[110] Shelley sent copies of this excellent pamphlet to Nugent, Burdett and a vigorous spokesman for reform in the Lords, Lord Stanhope. Seventy-five copies went to a London publisher, Thomas Hookham, who did not distribute them, perhaps because of the controversial content. Unfortunately, the remaining copies were never distributed either because of the subsequent events in Devon and the printer, Syle, destroyed them.[111]

Hitchener arrived in Devon, and, as she was undoubtedly still being 'watched', government spies were probably aware that she, Shelley and Healy were distributing Shelley's *Declaration of Rights* and his poem *The Devil's Walk*, which satirised the government and the Prince Regent. They flyposted, launched copies in bottles into the sea or in an air balloon, but probably more frequently handed the literature to people as they had done in Dublin. On 19 August, Healy was arrested in Barnstaple. Healy said that he was Shelley's servant, and that a stranger had paid him to distribute the pamphlets. When Shelley arrived, the authorities were suspicious as he did not appear to be surprised or angry with his 'servant'. Healy was sentenced to six months in prison since Shelley could not pay the £200 fine. He did pay 15 shillings a week so that Healy could be comfortable. The Mayor made enquiries about Shelley at Lynmouth and wrote to the Home Office. Lord Chichester, who had made the report on Hitchener, was once again involved and said he thought Shelley's family had 'suffer[ed] enough already from his conduct'. The Town Clerk was ordered to 'watch' Shelley, but by the time he arrived in Lynmouth, the group had left.[112]

3

Tremadog, Queen Mab *and the 'Hermit of Marlow': 1813–18*

S helley, Harriet, Hitchener and Eliza ended up in Tremadog, North Wales, a model town planned by William Madocks, the radical MP and supporter of Burdett who had proposed the impeachment of the Prime Minister and Foreign Secretary for corruption.[1] In 1798, Madocks had, by building a simple embankment across an inlet, reclaimed Traeth Mawr, 1,000 acres of sandy ground formerly covered by sea at high tide. The embankment opened with an ox roast, Eisteddfod, balls and plays and by 1803, crops were growing, there were farms and orchards, a woollen factory, fulling and corn mills. Madocks was a genial, pleasure-loving man who believed that 'in religion and education all should have fair play'. Tremadog therefore was built with a chapel and school as well as a church and a 'beautifully proportioned' town hall designed to double as an open air theatre. Facilities included shops, an inn, a town privy 'in Gothic style', a canal, roads and a race course. In 1812 a breach caused the sea to pour in.

Although he eventually got out of his difficulties, Madocks had run out of money and could not raise more or sell his property because of the economic crisis. At this point he could not meet the wages and the men went on strike. Shelley refers to their plight in the Notes to *Queen Mab*. Madocks did pay them as soon as he could, and, although local people had been initially unsupportive, they were now eager to help. Offers poured in from rich and poor alike.[2] Shelley pledged £100 towards rebuilding the embankment and helped John Williams, Madocks's devoted agent, raise funds from the local gentry. He went to London in October 1812 to raise more. There he at last met Godwin, his wife, Mary Jane, and their family on several occasions, sometimes with Harriet, Eliza and Hitchener, dining with him six times.[3]

The Godwins were children's publishers. Mary Jane had experience of working in the field and the originality and imagination of their books matched those of more prosperous businesses, especially their series of picture books of rhymes and tales, 'Copperplate Books'. The most elegant of these was the hand-coloured *Beauty and The Beast* (1813) which incorporated a pull-out sheet, '"Beauty a Song of her Spinning Wheel" set to Music by Mr. Whitaker'. The Godwins had authors like Coleridge and Charles and Mary Lamb on their list, not to mention Godwin himself, who wrote a two-volume *Fables Ancient and Modern* for children in a way which influenced subsequent versions. Godwin imagined 'taking the child upon my knee' (p. A2), and probably field-tested them on his own family of five since his stepson's name, Charles, appears more than once (pp. 6, 51–55). There were illustrations at the head of each chapter which were reproduced in a reduced size in the cheaper one-volume edition. Godwin had intended the fables to be educational, describing things that a child may not have come across: a lark (pp. 73–4), shellfish (pp. 117–18) or how to find the north (pp. 124–5) and pointing out a moral such as 'the brothers learned a lesson of diligence from this adventure' (p. 72). Despite the quality, however, the Godwins were unfortunate in finances after their first manager absconded with their money.[4]

Both the publishing and the Tremadog schemes were run commercially as that was the only means of achieving their aims in 1812, but they had progressive, social aims and were set up by people whose politics Shelley sympathised with. Although from a profit-making point of view they were unsuccessful, both had a lasting impact. The Tremadog area became a thriving port important for regional produce and the town is now frequently studied by architects and town planners. The Godwins published two books which have never been out of print, Charles and Mary Lamb's *Tales from Shakespear* (1807) and Johann David Wyss's *Swiss Family Robinson* (*The Family Robinson Crusoe*), 1814–16. Shelley's support for these activities stemmed from his broad political commitment.

Shelley contacted Hogg before they left London and they also parted with Hitchener. Harriet told Catherine Nugent that Hitchener 'built all her hopes on being able to separate me from my dearly beloved Percy'. It is unlikely that Hitchener would have had such plans. Shelley had made it quite clear to her before she decided to join them that his interest in her was not sexual but as an intellectual and political comrade. This was emphasised by his blunt remark when Hitchener told him that there was gossip in Sussex that she was to be his mistress. Shelley replied that no one would believe this as he had 'made a Scotch marriage with a woman who is handsome'.[5] Although Hitchener may not have been unattractive, he now described her as 'an ugly hermaphroditical beast', defending himself against any suggestion that she was a sexual threat to his relationship with Harriet. Although Harriet had written enthusiastically to Nugent both of Hitchener's character and her devotion to Ireland and 'the good of mankind' only two months earlier, she now said, 'We were entirely deceived [. . .] as to her republicanism'. Shelley's first attempt at living communally had failed and the household, which returned to Wales in mid-November, was again reduced to Shelley, Harriet and Eliza.[6]

The Shelleys lived in Madocks's own house, Tanyrallt, for which they were not asked to pay rent until Shelley's twenty-first birthday, August 1813, when he expected to come into some money. Shelley described the area as 'the last stronghold of serfdom'. This may not have been much of an exaggeration since 'Wales still had a social structure which was completely different from that in England where the middle classes had been steadily growing'.[7] Robert Leeson, an 'envious, unfeeling' landowner and quarry owner, was the brother of the Earl of Milltown, one of the wealthiest men in Ireland and the grandson of the Dean of Armagh, the 'centre of the Protestant Ascendancy'. According to Harriet, Leeson was heard to say that he would drive Shelley out of the country. In Ireland, she said, Shelley had made enemies who would 'execute their vengeance upon him' by having him arrested. Leeson told Shelley he had heard of him speaking at O'Connell's meeting and that he had obtained 'a pamphlet [. . .] containing matter dangerous to the state' from Williams and had it 'sent up to Government'.[8] This 'pamphlet' was more likely to have been the *Declaration of Rights* than either of the less appropriate *Address* or *Proposals*. He was already running out of the *Address* in

Ireland, he had distributed the *Declaration* in Lynmouth and was probably distributing it in Tremadog.[9]

Shelley was with Williams, 'in the office from morning till night'. He travelled round the country to raise money to 'send men & materials to repair' the embankment and made numerous gifts of food, clothes and fuel to poor people in the area.[10] Indeed, there was never a period when he was so busy, as he was writing in what time was left available. He began to study classical texts and history, recommended by Godwin and by his new friend, Thomas Love Peacock. On 15 February, he described *Queen Mab* as 'finished & transcribed' and he was 'preparing the Notes' and 'a Volume of Minor Poems'.[11] He invited another new friend, the publisher Hookham, and Hogg to visit, and, despite the 'Embankment affairs', he said, 'when I come home to Harriet I am the happiest of the happy.'[12] They were expecting their first child.

Biographers disagree as to whether an incident on the very stormy, rainy night of 26 February was a frightening attack by an intruder, a hallucination, a hoax contrived to allow him to leave Tanyrallt without paying his debts or a combination of the last two. From Harriet's account to Hookham, written a fortnight later, they were already in bed when they heard a noise. Shelley went downstairs, armed with two pistols, to find a man getting out through the French windows who fired at him. There was a struggle and Shelley thought he had wounded the intruder. Healy had just arrived from Devon, and they sat up for three hours when another attack occurred. Shelley was very shocked and 'in a nervous state'. The following day they left and went to stay with the Solicitor General, David Ellis-Nanney, and his wife for a few days before going to Killarney in Ireland.[13]

The first person to claim that Shelley invented the incident to allow him to leave the area without paying his debts was Leeson, the very next day; a strange thing for him to trouble to do unless he wanted doubt thrown on the event. Yet to stage one attack, let alone two, as an excuse to escape debt seems over-elaborate. Shelley's quarterly allowance was due to arrive within the month and, although he never managed to pay all his debts in Tremadog, including the £100 to the Embankment fund, he did pay some of them so it does not appear that he intended to avoid paying. Had he wanted an excuse, he could have said Harriet wished to have the baby near her family, which is what later happened. Also, if Shelley had successfully got himself out of a hole, he would have been cock-a-hoop, and the mood would have been evident eventually, even if he successfully masked it at first. Instead he appears to have had a nervous breakdown for several weeks which convinced not only Eliza, who described the event as 'a frightful fact', but the Ellis-Nanneys, with whom he stayed. Ellis-Nanney was later angry with Shelley for saying untruthfully that Ellis-Nanney had sold the furniture at Tanyrallt, but even then he did not suggest that either Shelley's attack or his illness were faked. Shelley told fantasy stories, experienced hallucinations and dramatised or exaggerated events when writing to friends, but this attack was a prolonged series of events which took place over nearly six hours which Harriet and Eliza corroborated. It does not seem likely it was imagined or faked.[14]

Shelley's friend, Peacock, described the attack as a 'semi-delusion', an opinion followed by Hogg and Medwin, none of whom were present. Although it is possible to pick holes in Harriet's account, unsurprisingly since both she and Shelley were upset, the explanations of those supporting the 'delusion' or 'fake' theories are also weak; it is hardly likely, for example, that 'Shelley held out his gown with one hand and fired through it with the other, the bullet then piercing the curtain and the wainscot' as Cameron suggests.[15] If details are unclear or even exaggerated, it does not mean that the incident never happened. The hallucination theory was established by 1820 when John Williams told his wife that the attack was imagined, but in 1813 he must have believed that it was not, as Madocks asked him why Shelley should have minded 'such a contemptible trick [. . .] to get him out of the Country on account of his liberal principles'.[16] Those who support the delusion theory refer to similarities in novels and poetry, including Shelley's own, and a sketch Shelley made on a fire-screen of his attacker, a devil with horns, but it is unwise to draw conclusions from fiction and the sketch was probably a black joke. They also mention an occurrence in Keswick when Shelley was knocked senseless by an intruder when he went to the door of his cottage. Although some local people disbelieved this, Shelley's landlord had pursued the attacker and would have contradicted a report in the local paper if it had been untrue.[17]

In rural areas, attacks, fires and burglaries are much discussed and different theories presented. A rural employer of wealth and standing like Leeson, even in the twenty-first century, is seldom criticised or opposed since local jobs and businesses depend on them, which is probably why Williams gave Leeson Shelley's pamphlet. Describing the attack as a delusion allowed Williams to throw doubt on it without supporting Leeson's story, and later Shelley's reputation as an eccentric added to its authority. Leeson may not have arranged the attack, but he had the means and the motive to do so. The government depended on civilian co-operation in repressing political opponents and Leeson may have been one of these co-operators.[18] Shelley had been kept under surveillance in Devon, but Chichester, and perhaps others, were reluctant to embarrass Shelley's father, so they may have contrived this way of silencing him. Whoever was responsible, Leeson did see Shelley driven out of the area. Eliza wrote to Williams saying they could not return because of the 'unpleasant scenes' and, after resting at Killarney in Ireland, she and the Shelleys went to London where Shelley finished adding the notes to *Queen Mab*. Their daughter, Eliza Ianthe, was born on 23 June.[19]

The war with France was coming to an end. Wellesley had gained victories at Salamanca (1812) and Vittoria (1813). In 1810, the Tsar had broken the Continental System, Bonaparte invaded Russia though the eventual retreat from Moscow destroyed his army. The occupied countries were dissatisfied not only at conscription but at being obliged to support an army which lived off the land. One of the reasons for Wellesley's success in Spain was that the British army lived off their own provisions, if necessary, supplied by the Royal Navy. The Confederation of the Rhine, which had been supportive of France, was dissolved. Bonaparte was defeated at the Battle of Leipzig and by spring 1813 had lost Italy and Holland. In France, his marshals refused to serve him, there were counter-revolutionaries, and the nation wanted peace.[20]

Unlike many radicals who opposed the war, Shelley himself had always been clear that Bonaparte was a tyrant who had betrayed the French Revolution. He described him to Hogg, on 27 December 1812, as 'hateful & despicable' and 'contemptible'. In Shelley's sonnet 'Feelings of a Republican on the Fall of Napoleon' (1815), he makes it clear that he hated him for his tyranny. Many of the poems which Shelley wrote between 1810–13 show his political views, for example, 'To Liberty', 'On Robert Emmet's Tomb' and 'To the Republicans of North America', which glorified the recent Mexican revolution. Many are against war, religion, monarchy, and tyranny, including Bonaparte's. 'A Tale of Society as it is' extends the anti-war theme to the plight of the impoverished and disabled returned soldier. His love poems to Harriet mention his equal love for political action and thought. These 'minor poems' would have formed a collection. They were written into a notebook kept by Harriet which passed to her descendants and were first published as a whole by Kenneth Neill Cameron in 1964 as *The Esdaile Notebook*.

Shelley attempted another reconciliation with his father, but Timothy still made the condition that he should retract his opinions. He did not receive the inheritance he had been expecting when he reached 21, although as he ascertained from T.C. Medwin, he was still heir to the estate. He had recently bought a carriage and he had a new baby and Harriet to support and numerous debts. His close association with Godwin had drawn him into the Godwins' financial difficulties. Godwin and Shelley were attempting to alleviate these by borrowing money on Shelley's future expectations. The interest on these 'post-obit bonds', as they were called, was exorbitant but they did not have to be paid until Shelley inherited his estate. Nevertheless, Shelley needed money himself, and it would not be surprising if both Eliza and Harriet had thought that his own debts should be paid first, particularly as he could be imprisoned for debt. Although Shelley believed Harriet was 'very happy as we are', her letters to Catherine Nugent express initial excitement at the idea of meeting his parents, and then anxiety over the possibility of Shelley's being disinherited.[21]

Shelley had 250 copies of *Queen Mab* published privately because the publisher thought it would be liable to prosecution. It is a narrative poem in which the fairy queen of the title appears to the spirit of a young sleeping woman, Ianthe, and takes her on a voyage through the universe in a magical car to show her the past, present and future. Mankind can learn from history and reason and make sure the future is quite unlike the tragic past. Shelley's notes emphasise that this is more than a mere utopian vision. Some notes draw on his own experience, for instance, that 'some of the workmen on an embankment in North Wales, who, in consequence of the inability of the proprietor to pay them, seldom received their wages, have supported large families by cultivating small spots of sterile ground by moonlight', adding, 'the peasantry work, not only for themselves, but for the aristocracy, the army, and the manufacturers'. Other notes drew from Godwin, Paine and Constantin-François, Comte de Volney, whose *Ruins of Empire* inspired many in the French Revolution.[22] Shelley later disliked notes in a poem and became less fond of *Queen Mab* as he wrote other poems, though he always defended its ideas. He had become a vegetarian in Ireland and his note 'On a Vegetable Diet' suggests that eating meat is unnatural to man since the non-carnivorous orang-utan is man's nearest relative. Although some of his claims for vegetarianism are far-fetched, his warning about contaminated water has since proved to be true and many agree with his point that grazing land could be more economically used for cultivation (in fact, this was done in England during the Second World War).[23]

Shelley had based his note partly on the work of John Newton, who had written a book showing that a vegetarian diet could be practical and nutritious. In November 1812, Shelley met Newton when he took Godwin's son, William, to a fireworks party at Newton's house. Newton's sister-in-law, Harriet Boinville, was married to a French revolutionary who died on the retreat from Moscow in February 1813. Boinville gathered round her a politically radical circle in Bracknell, Berkshire, including local working people and the Shelleys moved to Bracknell to be near her in June 1813. In the autumn, because of the danger of Shelley being arrested for debt, they revisited the Lake District and Edinburgh with Peacock. Harriet wrote to Nugent that the two years with Shelley had been the happiest of her life but, on their return south, she and Shelley began to spend more time apart. In February 1814, Shelley was staying at Boinville's house. In March, the Shelleys regularised their marriage with a church wedding and Harriet conceived a new baby, but while this is an apparent sign of rec-onciliation it can be the 'last chance' action of a failing relationship; in any case the money lenders required their marriage to be legal.[24]

Figure 5 Queen Mab by Portbury from the title page to *Percy Bysshe Shelley* (London: John Brooks, 1829). (Photograph by William Alderson, kind permission of Nora Crook)

Marriage Difficulties

Why this once happy relationship should have been on the rocks is not clear. Godwin's elder stepdaughter, Fanny, had described Harriet as a 'fine lady', but Shelley had rejected this although no doubt she seemed one to the Godwins. They had always been poor and made their own clothes which Claire Clairmont, Mary Jane's daughter, was later to remember Shelley had admired for their simplicity. Hogg hinted that Harriet became more interested in fashion after the return from Scotland, but Peacock thought that problems arose when Harriet refused to breastfeed Ianthe. Peacock tells an unbelievable story of how Shelley was so upset he attempted to breastfeed the child himself. Although this suggests that Shelley was the crank, it was Harriet who held an exceptionally old-fashioned view. Most mothers since the 1790s had considered breastfeeding the healthiest option and the idea that a 'lady' gave her child to a wet-nurse to feed was out of date. It is difficult to see why Harriet, at only nineteen, should have harked back to the eighteenth century unless there was a health reason or unless she was influenced by an older woman with more rigid views, perhaps Eliza.

Both Peacock and Hogg blame Eliza for the problems in the marriage and Shelley may have come to resent her influence. In March, Shelley wrote to Hogg explaining that he and Harriet had quarrelled over Eliza remaining with them. He adds that he hated to see 'her caress my poor little Ianthe, in whom I may hereafter find the consolation of sympathy' hinting that he did not get it from Harriet. In April, Boinville wrote to Hogg saying that 'Shelley's 'mind and body want rest' and that he was '*again* [my emphasis] a widower; his beauteous half went to town on Thursday with Miss Westbrook who is gone to live, I believe, at Southampton'.[25] Shelley had given up Hogg and Hitchener and perhaps Healy, who left in summer 1813, for Harriet's sake.[26] Why Eliza remained so long is not exactly clear. She perhaps wanted to protect her sister in this financially and politically unstable situation, but although it may not have been her intention to find herself a husband of a similar status through her sister's marriage, she did find one.

Shelley's preoccupation and unhappiness is suggested by how little he wrote, compared to the previous winter, completing only a few poems and *A Refutation of Deism* which takes the form of a dialogue between a Christian and a Deist. Each argues to defend their belief, but in so doing the weaknesses of both ideologies are exposed. Shelley states in the preface that his object is 'to show there is no alternative between atheism and Christianity', but it is clear that atheism is preferable to either. Instead of stating it bluntly, he used a more subtle approach which was not only more acceptable but also less liable to prosecution.[27]

From May 1814, Shelley frequently visited London to negotiate with the moneylenders over his 'post-obit bonds' and then he dined with the Godwins. Mary, the daughter of Godwin and Wollstonecraft, had returned from a year in Scotland. Godwin described her as 'very pretty, singularly bold, somewhat imperious, and active of mind'. She was also probably aware of her attractiveness; Robert Baxter, the son of the family with whom she had lived in Scotland, was in love with her and is believed to have proposed. When Shelley fell in love with her is not certain, but Hogg's account suggests that they met secretly. On 23 June, Ianthe's first birthday, Shelley tried once again to rent Nangtwillt, perhaps with the hope of saving his marriage with Harriet, as he begged Godwin to allow him to return to Bracknell. Godwin would not let him go until his loan had been sorted out by which time Harriet had left Bracknell for Bath. On 26 June, Mary declared her love for Shelley and it was this honesty, courage and unconventional behaviour which was the decisive factor, as he later told Hogg, in his commitment to her. When Shelley told Godwin of his love for Mary, Godwin banned him from the house and Mary promised not to see him, but they secretly corresponded.[28] Shelley met Harriet in London and wrote to her in gratitude for her understanding, saying he was still attached to her but that, as Boinville had pointed out, their love was on the basis of friendship not 'all sufficing passion'.[29]

With or without an 'all sufficing passion', Shelley and Harriet had spent two years together, had one child and another on the way. Harriet was in an impossible situation. At the age of nineteen, with no possibility of divorce, she was neither married nor unmarried and could not remarry. Harriet told Nugent that Mary had suggested that they all lived together, she as his wife and Harriet as his sister. This may have been a practical solution but Harriet considered it out of the question, as many women would do. If she wished to be thought 'respectable', she could only live at home with her parents, a life which she found miserable and which she had rejected when she married Shelley.[30] It was unforgivable of him to leave her when she was carrying his child and so to withdraw the protection which they had believed he would give her by marriage. But Shelley was no longer happy with her and appears to have believed that she no longer loved him, or perhaps had never done. He was not prepared to give up his love for Mary, who was highly intelligent, imaginative and creative. They were well-suited. He was to write to Mary, 'My mind without yours is dead & cold as the dark midnight river when the moon is down'.[31] Peacock remembered Shelley's near-suicidal sufferings in this dilemma. At the same time, Harriet was 'laid up' for two weeks and Shelley 'begged her to live'.[32]

On 28 July 1814, Shelley and Mary eloped to France, taking with them Mary's stepsister, Claire Clairmont, who spoke French fluently. Claire herself said that she had accompanied them for that reason – also probably for the adventure. They left her alone on the journey, as they had done when she went for walks with them in London, since they were completely wrapped up in each other. They were not a threesome, although Shelley may have hoped to set up a new community to include Claire and perhaps Harriet whom he invited to join them in France. Bonaparte had abdicated on 6 April 1814 and Louis XVIII had been restored. A Congress of Vienna, whose British representative was Castlereagh, was deciding the future of the rest of Europe. The civilian population in France had initially offered no resistance to the allied troops as they were so war-weary, but then the Cossack and Prussians arrived and burnt villages and raped and murdered the inhabitants. While travelling through northern France, Shelley, Mary and Claire saw wrecked cottages and met a man whose child had been murdered by the Cossacks. In Paris they met a royalist who boasted that he had bribed the 'mob' to overthrow Bonaparte. They got as far as Switzerland, but by that time they had run out of money and had to return to England, first travelling down the Rhine by boat, where they argued with someone about the slave trade. They were obliged to borrow money from Harriet to pay a boatman who took them from Gravesend to London.[33]

During the autumn, Shelley often communicated with Harriet, but Mary expressed jealousy of her, especially when Harriet gave birth to a son, Charles. Shelley was being pursued for debt and he gave no financial support to Harriet and the children. He and Mary were very short of money. They moved lodgings frequently and were often parted while Shelley avoided the bailiffs. Godwin refused to see them or to allow other members of his family to do so. Mary had a premature baby on 22 February, a little girl, who lived only until 6 March.[34]

Their relationship was never to be completely exclusive and this may be one reason why Shelley thought it would be more successful than his marriage with Harriet. Although Claire reports Mary weeping when Shelley had suggested she should sleep with Hogg, he would have left it to Mary to choose, given his attitude towards Hogg's behaviour with Harriet. Mary decided that she 'like[d] him [Hogg] better than before' and she wrote him some flirtatious letters.[35] Hogg was a comfort to Mary when her baby died but their relationship appears to have ended when the Shelleys went away for a few days together. Some suggest that Claire and Shelley had a sexual relationship but, despite their affection for each other, there is no real evidence for this. It is inferred from Mary's desire not to have Claire living with them and by ambiguous remarks in letters or journals. Mary, however, did not want Claire to stay with her even after Shelley's death because they were never compatible, despite being fond of each other. Shelley and Mary moved without Claire to Bishopsgate, near Windsor, during 1815 and their son, William, was born in January 1816.[36]

Alastor

In 1815, Shelley took up boating again and sailed up the Thames in a wherry with Peacock as far as Lechlade.[37] Shelley also worked on his next long published poem, *Alastor, or the Spirit of Solitude* which was quite unlike *Queen Mab*. In *Alastor*, a Poet is devoted to Nature and to learning and he voyages to Africa and Kashmir where he learns wisdom. His is an anti-racist, anti-imperialist attitude. However, he realises that he also needs human sympathy. He dreams of a woman who is his ideal and begins to search for her, whilst ignoring a real Arab maiden who loves him and who brings him things from her father's tent, just as Mary Godwin brought resources from her upbringing which enriched Shelley's life. He sees the ideal reflection everywhere: the Spirit which seems to stand beside him and hold commune with him beckons him with eyes of stars (487–90); and the stream which he travels down images his life (502–05). In the Preface, Shelley points out that 'among those who attempt to exist without human sympathy, the pure and tender-hearted perish through the intensity and passion of their search after its communities' but the furies pursue the poet for his 'self-centred seclusion' and bring about his death (pp. 92–3). The Poet has high ideals in morals and politics, but he cannot live in solitude.

The poem is in part a response to Wordsworth, whose poetry Shelley had greatly admired. In *The Excursion*, Wordsworth avowed that the proper course for a poet was to live in solitude and write, not to be involved in political activity. After reading *The Excursion*, Mary Shelley remarked, 'He is a slave', meaning voluntarily surrendering to another's authority as distinct from being forced into slavery. It was no doubt also Shelley's opinion and the Wordsworthian style of *Alastor* emphasises the connection. However, Shelley wrote other poems which expressed his views about Wordsworth's change of heart and *Alastor* is more than this, it is about the education of a poet. It is not just the love of Nature which leads the Poet to his solitary doom, but the love of learning, both of which could easily seduce Shelley himself. Godwin had encouraged Shelley's reading but discouraged his political activity: *Alastor* suggests that if a poet rejects political life, it will lead to poetic death. Shelley had not rejected political commitment, but he had found another arena and another way of writing.

Shelley had difficulty in finding a publisher. He initially sent the poem to John Murray, who was later to describe Shelley as 'the vilest wretch in existence'. He sent presentation copies to all the famous poets of the day including Southey, George Gordon, Lord Byron and Leigh Hunt. Literary journals took up clear political stances and they fought dirty. Writers were willy-nilly put into political camps. The *Quarterly Review* was emphatically Tory, and was later to attack Shelley. *Blackwood's Edinburgh Magazine* had attacked 'Cockney Poets', like Leigh Hunt and John Keats, as if they had no right to write poetry but they eventually gave *Alastor* an excellent review.[38]

Quakers and Spenceans

At Bishopsgate, Shelley knew a Quaker, 68-year-old Dr Robert Pope, who said 'I like to hear thee talk, friend Shelley; I see thee art very deep'. Peacock gives the impression that Pope and Shelley were discussing 'theology', but this is probably a misunderstanding; Quakers are less dependent on theological dogma than other religious groups, although Robert Barclay's (1648–90) theories had led to eighteenth-century Quakers becoming a strict sect, opposing marriage outside Quaker families and considering time spent on the arts a waste. Shelley would have found these aspects unacceptable but he shared the Quaker principles of equality, justice, truth and peace and lived in Quaker simplicity. Quakers have been interested since the seventeenth century in ways of solving conflict peacefully and were proud of the role the Irish Friends had played in 1798. They had destroyed their hunting guns so that they could not take sides, acted as mediators and intervened to prevent executions of 'rebels'. Dr Abraham Shackleton, of Ballitore, Co. Kildare, was taken away by rebels and threatened with being used as a human shield but he avoided this, probably because of their respect for him. His house was a haven for both sides throughout the conflict. Pope and Shelley are likely to have discussed these matters in view of Shelley's visit to Ireland and his interest in Quaker principles.[39]

Mary Shelley was to write that Shelley's 'inclinations led him (he fancied) almost alike to poetry and metaphysical discussions' and this is supported by Shelley's 1819 letter to Peacock. She believed, however, that poetry was paramount and Shelley was now to devote more of his time to poetry, perhaps through Mary's influence or perhaps because he felt his health was not good enough to risk another attack such as he had suffered at Tremadog, but politics remained very important to him.[40] In 1815, he arranged with George Cannon, a Spencean who edited the *Theological Inquirer*, to publish extracts from *Queen Mab* which reached a wider and more radical audience than Shelley would have reached otherwise. Shelley did not like Cannon, describing him as a 'vulgar brute', but he had a long discussion with him on philosophy which would have been likely to have included Thomas Spence's ideas.

Spence had died in 1814. He was a teacher from Newcastle who had been expelled from its Philosophical Society in 1775 for reading a paper entitled *The Real Rights of Man*. His scheme of land reform went further than Paine's *Agrarian Justice*; he considered all land should be owned by parishes and the income should be divided equally among people whether or not they worked on the land. In London he became a leader of the London Corresponding Society (LCS) and sold his journal *Pig's Meat* which included extracts from British and French philosophers and political writers, and his own *Rights of Man* as well as Paine's. Paine had believed in private property, but Spence believed that if the aristocracy would not give up their land it should be seized, although they should be allowed to keep articles such as jewellery or carriages. He stood for religious toleration, a free press, abolition of slavery and was against marriage. When political meetings became illegal, Spence's followers met in taverns at less obviously political 'free and easies' consisting of songs mixed with education in the 'truth'. They attracted mechanics and 'manufacturers' (factory workers) along with former soldiers and sailors. The Spenceans were organised in groups in the manner of the LCS and possibly had links with similar groups in cities such as Sheffield and Manchester; former Jacobins joined them. After Spence's death, Thomas Evans, who had been imprisoned in Cold Bath Fields in the 1790s, became the organiser. While preserving the informality of the meetings, Evans instituted a joining fee, debating procedures and published Spence's work. He adapted Spence's plan in his *Christian Polity*, a work Malthus denounced in his *Essay on the Principle of Population* which Shelley knew.[41]

Geneva

In March 1816, Claire began an affair with Byron, and she persuaded Shelley and Mary to go for the summer to Geneva where he was living. Byron's maiden speech in the House of Lords had been against the Framebreaking Bill and he had presented Cartwright's petition for reform in 1813. The poets became friends. They saw each other nearly every day and went on a boat trip over Lake Lucerne together. Canto III of Byron's *Childe Harold* is said to show Shelley's intellectual influence. It was here that Mary began her novel *Frankenstein* and Shelley wrote the poems *Hymn to Intellectual Beauty* and *Mont Blanc*. These were published in *The Examiner*, introduced by Leigh Hunt. This led to a close and lasting friendship with Hunt giving Shelley good publicity while Shelley supported Hunt financially. Shelley now became part of a literary circle which included the radical theatre critic and journalist William Hazlitt and the poets John Keats and Horace Smith. Smith and his brother had written a popular comic parody of modern poets, *Rejected Addresses*. Smith had been a stockbroker but he shared many of Shelley's views: he thought war 'an act of national madness' and poverty 'the greatest of evils'. Shelley remarked, 'Odd that Smith the only true generous person I ever knew, who had money to be generous with, should be a stockbroker!'[42]

Smith was later to help Shelley manage his financial affairs, and the friendship was also to prove important artistically. Shelley and he competed to write a sonnet on the same subject, and Shelley's was one of his best-known short – and political – poems, *Ozymandias*. Smith described Shelley as 'fair, freckled, blue-eyed light-haired, delicate looking' with 'a beaming countenance' and 'fragile frame', 'of extensive reading and undoubted genius', who 'felt [. . .] a devout reverence for what he believed to be the truth', 'a moral Quixote'. Mary Shelley too referred to her husband as 'Don Quixote'.[43]

Harriet's Death

Shelley's financial situation had eased when his grandfather died in January 1815 and his income was increased to £1,000. Out of this, he had allowed Harriet £200 annually, but when she asked for more Shelley requested custody of Ianthe. Harriet refused, citing Shelley's religious principles. She had threatened to prosecute Shelley for atheism 'if he did not make a handsome settlement on her' and would not agree to a deed of separation. It is not clear why. Like Shelley, Henry ('Orator') Hunt married young against his family's wishes but later met Mrs Vince who became his lifelong companion and in that case his wife agreed to a separation.[44] In Shelley's case, there followed the sad but unfortunately common squabble about money and custody.[45]

On returning to England, Shelley heard of Harriet's death. She had moved away from her father's house and had become pregnant. Believing herself abandoned by her lover, thought to be a soldier in India, she had committed suicide by drowning in the Serpentine. Shelley wanted custody of Ianthe and Charles, but the Westbrooks refused and settled money on them, so that the case was fought in the Chancery Court. To help win the case, Shelley married Mary in December 1816. The ceremony was 'so magical in its effects' that Godwin was now reconciled and even helped Shelley with his legal arguments. The Westbrooks produced *Queen Mab* as evidence that Shelley was an atheist and against marriage, and he lost the legal battle. The judge was Lord Eldon. The children were not placed with any relation but with a clergyman and his wife. The effect that this must have had upon them is easily surmised. It was a great source of grief to Shelley and, as he told Byron, he feared his other children might be taken from him too.[46]

The debate over the rights and wrongs of Shelley's separation from Harriet is still controversial 200 years later. In the nineteenth century, those such as William Rossetti, who desired to exculpate Shelley made unproven, indefensible accusations of drunkenness and adultery against Harriet, but after the 1930 publication of Shelley's letters to her used by the Westbrooks in the custody case, the tendency has been to condemn Shelley alone for the break-up. Some of Shelley's remarks in these letters were tactless and unsympathetic in the extreme, but as there are none of Harriet's letters to him we do not know what provocation he was responding to. After Shelley left her, Harriet showed a normal, angry reaction in her letters to Nugent and she fought over custody and financial issues. She was spirited and attractive and had at least one other relationship after the separation. The Victorian stereotype has been discarded for another, the passive victim.

Shelley was against marriage because the marriage laws were deeply misogynist, requiring a woman to obey her husband. He was one of the earliest advocates of freedom for women, both sexual and intellectual, and he encouraged both Harriet and Mary to study and develop their ideas. Harriet's tragedy was not solely because of her separation from Shelley, but because of contemporary attitudes towards marriage and divorce and the situation of single parents, attitudes which leave their mark on relationships in the twenty-first century.

In February 1817, the Shelleys settled at Albion House, Marlow, close to Peacock. Claire and her baby, later called Allegra, joined them and in September the Shelleys had a daughter, Clara. The Godwins, Leigh and Marianne Hunt and Horace Smith visited them there. Shelley led a quiet life: rising early, eating frugally and writing his poem *Laon and Cythna* in his boat. Although it was an idyllic summer with picnicking in the woods and boating, the house in winter was damp, and Shelley's health suffered. The 'house was very political as well as poetical' and Shelley and Peacock were considering boycotting paying tax, a form of protest later called for by the huge Smithfield meeting in 1819 following the 'Peterloo Massacre' and strongly supported by Henry Hunt.[47]

Political Agitation

Shelley was aware of the political crisis developing at the time. The end of the war had brought unemployment, and mechanisation meant that artisans were unable to making a living by their crafts. Small employers and farmers cut wages. Although wages had almost doubled, the cost of living had risen accordingly. The Enclosure Acts had caused common land and small-holdings to gradually disappear over the previous 50 years, but between 1809–15 the number of acts increased to one hundred a year. In Scotland, Highland landowners found that they could make money from pasturing sheep. Small cultivators whose families had tilled the land for centuries were thrown off and had to emigrate to the industrial towns or America. The national debt had swollen but the government reduced income tax, which affected the rich, while taxing necessities such as candles or soap, something Shelley remarks upon in his fragmentary essay *On the Game Laws*.[48] In 1815 the Corn Law was introduced, which made bread impossibly expensive for the poor. Discharged soldiers and sailors had no option but to join the beggars. Low pay, overwork and unemployment were increasing even in the well-organised trades. In 1816 Manchester spinners again went on strike, although this was crushed by the combination laws. Working people were beginning to believe that reform of Parliament might provide a solution.[49]

Although in 1816 the Hampden Clubs had grown enormously, the reform movement was divided. New radical journalists and leaders had sprung up, the most popular among them being William Cobbett, who supported parliamentary reform. Initially a Tory, he had been shaken by his treatment over his pamphlet *The Soldier's Friend* and his attempt to get redress for soldiers who were defrauded of their pay by their officers. He did not become radical, however, until 1810 when he was imprisoned for an article denouncing flogging in the army. Although newspapers were subject to stamp duty which put them out of reach of all but the wealthier classes, Cobbett started to issue the front page of his *Political Register* as a single sheet for 2d. The circulation in 1817 was 40,000.[50] Other radical newspapers were the *Black Dwarf* (Thomas Wooler), *The Reformist* (William Hone) and *Sherwin's Political Register* (which later became *The Republican*), edited by Richard Carlile. These journalists were to face numerous trials and imprisonment in their struggle against censorship.

In June 1816, the price of wheat suddenly rose and there were riots in many parts of the country; in Ely, Downham Market and Littleport in the Fens there was rebellion. Claire wrote to Byron that 'numerous vagrants . . . lie about the Streets of London, naked & starving' and 'the price of Bread is extremely high'. Marlow was also affected. Mary Shelley remarked that the bad harvest and post-war economic situation 'brought with them the most heart-rending evils to the poor' and that Shelley 'afforded what relief he could'. Claire gave one instance of this in her letter to Byron.[51]

In January 1817, Cartwright organised a meeting of delegates at the Crown and Anchor tavern, using O'Connell's way of getting round the sedition laws by declaring it open to the public. Cartwright was advocating universal suffrage and had great support in the industrial and Luddite areas whereas Burdett was now in favour of suffrage for all who paid 'direct taxes' (property owners) and was supported in this by the Westminster committee who were choosing Whig rather than radical candidates.[52]

The Spenceans arranged a demonstration of 'Distressed Manufacturers, Mariners, Artisans, and others' on 15 November 1816 in

Spa Fields to which they invited Henry Hunt to speak. They had planned a 'memorial' to the Prince Regent relating to the Spencean plan but Hunt changed it to be 'strictly constitutional'. Hunt regarded parliamentary reform as an end while the Spenceans saw it as just a beginning. When the meeting turned out to be huge beyond all expectations, Hunt spoke from a window overlooking the fields. It was agreed to have another meeting to give the Spenceans a chance to put their views on 2 December 1816. The committee included a spy, Castle, who reported to government that 'something was going to happen' since there was talk of an army mutiny and the Spa Fields banners proclaimed 'The brave soldiers are our friends, treat them kindly'. At this demonstration, a contingent led by 'young' Watson, a Spencean, attempted an attack on the Tower of London. There were riots. At the trial, the only evidence was from Castle, but Hunt spoke in the Spenceans' defence, saying that Castle had tried to drag Hunt himself into a plot. They were acquitted but the riots split the reform leaders.[53]

Burdett, although chair of the organising committee, did not attend the January meeting. 151 delegates brought petitions signed by half a million people and, since it would be Burdett who would present the petitions in Parliament, Cartwright advised them to demand household suffrage. Henry Hunt, however, stuck to universal suffrage. He and Cobbett broke with Burdett and persuaded Cochrane to present the petitions. Later that day, the Prince Regent's coach window was broken – as Claire remarked to Byron, 'the people are most enraged at the Prince'. The government used the excuse of an 'attempted rising' to suspend Habeas Corpus, forbid public meetings – even reading rooms had to be licensed – and impose drastic penalties for 'treasonable speech and writing'. At another Spa Fields meeting on 10 February, Hunt spoke once again, rejecting the Spencean plan, and saying he would lay down his life defending universal suffrage, annual parliaments and the ballot. Shelley intervened in the reform movement with *A Proposal for Putting Reform to the Vote*.[54]

This has been described as 'planting his banner firmly in the camp of the moderates' but, read with an awareness of Shelley's style in *A Refutation of Deism*, there are clues that Shelley is not doing this. Many of his remarks show his hatred for the system: 'the House of Commons' is 'not a representation of the people' but exercises sovereignty 'in contempt' of them in 'a hospital for lunatics'. By saying that 'people ought to legislate for themselves' he suggests that universal suffrage should be the goal, asking 'whether we are to be slaves or freemen', adding ironically 'perhaps the people choose to be enslaved'. His suggestion is another Crown and Anchor meeting with everyone in the country interested in reform either attending or sending letters. Britain should be divided into equal electoral districts (one of Cartwright's demands) in which each inhabitant should be asked to sign a declaration that Parliament does not represent the will of the People. If they are in the majority then the House of Commons should reform to make its members 'the actual representatives of the nation'. If Parliament refused to reform, 'Parliament would then have rebelled against the people' – as Charles I was said to have done, thereby causing the Civil War. Shelley says that these meetings should continue until the object is achieved and that they are not 'revolutionary'. In fact, if Shelley's plan were successful, as it would have been, given the enthusiasm for reform shown by the Hampden Club meetings, the country would have been in a revolutionary situation. Shelley does not state this directly and neither does he make it clear what the consequence would be of Parliament rebelling against the people.[55]

Two demands which divided the reformers were annual or triennial Parliaments and universal or limited suffrage. Shelley calls for unity around a demand from each programme once the referendum has been carried out: limited suffrage and annual Parliaments which would help 'familiarize men with liberty by disciplining them to an habitual acquaintance with its forms'. Shelley's desire for people to develop their own political ideas is similar to the approach of Marx and Lenin.[56] The consequence of this would be that with more people active in politics every year, demands for universal suffrage would increase – Shelley suggests proceeding gradually and with caution in order to avoid anarchy and despotism; he hopes to achieve a 'pure Republic' peaceably, which is shown in his discarded note cautioning against those who 'would abolish the Lords and pull down the King, careless of all the ruin and bloodshed that must ensue'. He may have remembered that the opponents of slavery had to moderate their demand to abolition of the slave trade to get it through Parliament. When Burdett presented a petition with all the demands for reform, only Cochrane supported him.[57]

Shelley sent his pamphlet to a number of reformers, including Cobbett and Robert Owen. He had not met Owen, but, as Owen had frequently visited Godwin since 1813 and was to visit again in March 1817, Shelley may have heard his views. At the time Owen had managed to get the House of Commons to appoint a committee to consider a Factory bill prohibiting employment of children under ten, limiting working hours to a maximum of ten and a half, forbidding night work for juniors and arranging instruction for children and requiring factory inspectors and doctors. Owen stated in his *Observations on the Effect of the Manufacturing System* (1816) that 30 years earlier 'the poorest peasants thought the age of fourteen sufficiently early for their children to commence regular labour;' that 'even for the most robust adults, the working day then never exceeded twelve hours, and holidays were far more frequent' and that 'they had also frequent opportunities for healthy, rational sports and amusements'. Under the factory system, however, children were employed in unhealthy surroundings and 'the employer regards the employed as mere instruments of gain'. He suggests that the inevitable result of this change will be revolution. Shelley echoes his language and views in his political writing.[58]

In the early part of 1817, informers were sending reports to government about an insurrection in the north. Arrests were made. The suspension of Habeas Corpus meant that people like Samuel Bamford, a radical cotton worker, were imprisoned indefinitely without having committed any offence. A group of cotton workers gathered in St Peter's Fields, Manchester, to march to London to present a petition, each carrying a blanket and hoping that other working families would provide hospitality on the way. Although no one had forbidden the march, the soldiers prevented it leaving and arrested the leaders, and those who had already left were arrested and imprisoned en route. Only one man reached London. In this atmosphere, a band of 300, including quarrymen, labourers and framework knitters, marched from Derbyshire villages to Nottingham. They were betrayed by the spy Oliver, captured by soldiers and tried for high treason by a packed jury with ten lawyers for the prosecution and only two for the defence. Although the *Leeds Mercury*, a paper strongly influenced by the Yorkshire reformers, later exposed Oliver, his name was inadmissible at the trial. Three leaders, Jeremiah Brandreth, William Turner and Isaac Ludlam, were hanged and then beheaded (they were spared drawing and quartering!). The coincidence of the news of these executions arriving on the same day as the death in childbirth of Princess Charlotte, the heir to the throne, inspired Shelley's *An Address to the People on the Death of the Princess Charlotte*. Cobbett remarked on the coincidence, saying that he had 'thought much more about poor Brandreth and Turner and Ludlam's death *which took place in the very same twentyfour hours*' and many thought that her death was a judgement from God over the execution. This was the starting point for Shelley's essay, but Shelley's goes much further.[59]

The opening of the *Address* strikes the note of expected sympathy with the death of the princess, but Shelley continues 'thousands of the poorest poor' suffer this calamity and women who are in 'penury and shame' die and leave no one who can look after their orphans. 'Have they no affections?' Public mourning might be justified if it commemorated those who had 'done some service' to the public or for states of national calamity. His examples of the first were John Milton, Voltaire and Rousseau, all opposed to tyranny (p.624), and of the second 'the extinguishing of the French Republic' and – reminding the reader of a former occasion when Habeas Corpus was suspended – if the LCS leaders had been executed. Brandreth, Turner and Ludlam had 'private virtues' (p. 625), perhaps more than the princess. The princess did nothing for the public while the events that led to the executions are a public calamity. Shelley comes close to expressing opposition to the death penalty under any situation.[60]

Then Shelley comes to his real point. Workers are getting no more for working 16 hours a day than they previously got for working eight, they are famished, without health, leisure or opportunity for education, yet there is a national debt, a standing army, a royal family and their hangers on. Inequality of wealth is worsened by a 'double aristocracy' of bankers and stockbrokers. When the public demands parliamentary representation, the government passes laws against 'sedition' and sends spies to trap men into a rebellion. 'How ought we not to mourn?' A 'beautiful princess' has died, Shelley concludes, 'LIBERTY'. Shelley's final sentence expresses an idea which he was to repeat in *The Mask of Anarchy*. British liberty, as it used to be, is now dead, but from this death, a new spirit may arise, one which will get rid of the old system of kings and war signified by swords, sceptres and crowns.[61]

Laon and Cythna

The theme of *Laon and Cythna*, the poem Shelley was working on during 1817, is also liberty.[62] Laon and Cythna are as passionate and politically committed as the poet of *Alastor* was detached; revolutionary leaders, symbolically equal as brother and sister and lovers. Laon inspires others through his defiance of the soldiers who kidnap Cythna for the harem of Othman, the ruling tyrant of the Golden City, and he suffers torture and near death, but his suffering and leadership pale before hers. Cythna is imprisoned in an underground cave for her own defiance of Othman, but she is released by an earthquake and is rescued by sailors. Their cargo is slave women bound for the harem. She persuades the sailors to release them. The liberation of the women in turn liberates the sailors, and once back in the Golden City, women and men both flock to hear Cythna. Laon hears of her in the hermit's retreat where he is being nursed back to health and goes to join her. They play leading roles in the revolution which deposes Othman. The revolutionaries spare him, and even give him a semblance of splendour, with the result that he mounts a counter-revolution, massacring the people. Cythna, on her black horse, rescues Laon from the battlefield and they have a few days of happiness and love. But Laon learns that famine and plagues have succeeded the massacres. The Christian priest allied to Othman persuades the people that their sufferings will only end if Laon and Cythna are sacrificed. Laon gives himself up on the condition that Cythna should be allowed to go to America, but Othman breaks his word (ll. 4549–4550) and Cythna joins Laon at the stake. At the sight of them dying together, Othman's daughter, Cythna's child, stolen from her in captivity, dies too. She had pleaded for Laon's life. Laon had seen her dancing for Othman in his defeat and had given her a fatherly kiss. The poem ends with an idyllic boat voyage along a wooded river to the Temple of Virtue.

Although Laon recounts the tale, the centre of the poem is Cythna, who is transformed from child, to slave girl, from prisoner to political leader and warrior. She has the most passionate and optimistic speeches, including the line 'Can man be free if woman be a slave?' (1045) In a prefiguring of Shelley's *Ode to the West Wind* she argues that though she and Laon have not been successful, the revolution will succeed one day, their lives are not wasted as their actions and thoughts will inspire others. Shelley believed that a revolution could succeed by winning over the soldiers to peace and Laon won over Othman's soldiers by sparing the life of one of them. But when they spare Othman, the revolutionaries are rewarded with counter-revolution. Shelley presents revolution as involving little bloodshed, but counter-revolution as savage. He was to repeat the warning that defeated tyrants cannot be trusted in *A Philosophical View of Reform*.

Shelley met Charles and James Ollier, who published *Laon and Cythna*, through Leigh Hunt. They were interested in publishing radical poetry, but when the printer, McMillan, who was printer to the Royal family, pointed out he was risking prosecution for blasphemous libel and a customer complained about the anti-religious aspects in *Laon and Cythna*, they wanted to withdraw it. Seven hundred and fifty copies had already been issued, Shelley had paid for the printing and it had been well advertised.[63] He invited Ollier to stay at Marlow and a 'committee', including Peacock, decided on how to alter the poem. In line with such alterations made to plays for performance at the time, the word 'God' was eliminated or changed to 'gods', implying a pagan religion, and words such as 'heaven's anger' were substituted for 'God's wrath'. Laon and Cythna's brother and sister relationship, which symbolised equality, was also changed and the title became *The Revolt of Islam*. At least the essential message was available for sympathetic readers to pick up. Peacock explains how Shelley resisted the changes, 'to the very end, always insisting his poem was spoiled', but 'his friends prevailed'. In 2013, a copy of *Laon and Cythna* was discovered with alterations by Peacock, confirming his account.[64] Shelley told Godwin that he had written it with all

Figure 6 Illustration to *The Revolt of Islam* Canto VI xxi from *The Poetical Works of Percy Bysshe Shelley* (London: Milne and Sowerby). *Then 'Away! Away!['] she cried and stretched her sword / As't were a scourge over the coursers head.* (Photograph by William Alderson, kind permission of Nora Crook)

his heart, wanting to 'leave something of myself', as he thought he might not have long to live.[65] His friend and physician, Lawrence, had diagnosed 'a consumptive disorder' (tuberculosis), and advised a warmer climate.

Although Shelley's financial affairs were better regulated after his union with the more practical Mary, he still had difficulty in calculating his expenses as Mary complained, and he was still in debt.[66] She also worried about Claire and Allegra living with them; gossip held that Allegra was Shelley's child and, although he did not mind gossip, Mary did. Byron, who was in Italy, had consented to bring Allegra up. Once the destination of the Grand Tour, Italy was now a place where English people were choosing to live because of the mild climate and the lower cost of living. The Shelleys decided to move to Italy.[67]

4

Italy and Shelley's Annus Mirabilis: 1818–19

Before 1796, Italy had comprised the republics of Venice, Genoa and Lucca, Dukedoms under Hapsburg rulers, the Papal States and two kingdoms, Piedmont-Sardinia and Naples united with Sicily, all with different currencies and laws. The 'enlightened' Grand Duke of Tuscany had introduced legal and administrative reforms. Bonaparte's army, smaller and less well-armed than the Austrians but with greater speed and flexibility, drove them out of northern Italy and by the Treaty of Campo Formio (1797) gained the whole peninsula. French forces were initially welcomed in their neighbouring countries and, since the Piedmontese regions of Savoy and Nice wanted union with France, there had been uprisings and in 1794 an attempt to overthrow the government, but the 'Jacobins' were weak and never gained the support of the peasants as they had in France. Bonaparte found the revolutionary movements useful against the old régimes but once Italy had become a base from which to launch attacks on Austria he imposed French control and put down rebellion.[1]

Some of the benefits the Revolution had brought to France were established: secularisation of church property and of education, equality before the law, freeing of serfs, religious toleration, civil rights for Jews, the civil code and civil marriage. The French built roads and canals, introduced standardised weights and measures and other reforms, many of which still exist today. Although the middle classes benefited from the job opportunities in the bureaucracy and army, the peasants did not and deeply resented both conscription and the army living off the land. In the Neapolitan Republic, the poor who no longer had church charity, blamed 'the Jacobins' for their hardship. After Bonaparte's *coup d'état* (1799) in which he made himself First Consul, the republics collapsed. Cardinal Ruffo led a bloody counter-revolution in Calabria, massacring 'Jacobins' and executing 100 republican leaders. Bonaparte returned in 1800 to create the Republic of Italy (Kingdom, when he became Emperor of the French in 1804). Bonaparte made his brother, Joseph, King of Naples but in 1808, Joseph became King of Spain and Joseph Murat took his place. Ferdinand IV held court in Sicily and Vittore Emanuele I in Sardinia, islands kept independent of France by the Royal Navy.[2]

In 1815, the Congress of Vienna not only allowed the Austrians to repossess what they had ruled before, but also gave Austria Venice and the right to intervene militarily in Italy if Austria's interests were threatened. The Pope got the Papal States back, Genoa was added to Piedmont-Sardinia and the kings returned to their kingdoms, causing resentment in the islands where they had held court. Both kings purged the civil service, demoted army officers and handed education to the Jesuits, thus alienating those who had become an élite under Bonaparte. In Tuscany, the Grand Duke was not as liberal as his predecessor had been.[3]

The Shelleys, who were eventually to settle in Tuscany, arrived in Piedmont, but spent only one night there before going on to Milan, which had been Bonaparte's capital. Since Milan had been so strongly progressive, it was difficult for the Austrians to suppress all dissent. There were still groups of liberals and former Jacobins and a liberal journal of economic, political and cultural affairs, *Il Conciliatore*, which was not suppressed by the Austrians until 1819 when those involved were arrested, exiled or, in the case of Silvio Pellico, spent ten years in prison. Although Byron knew some of them personally,[4] it is not likely that the Shelleys did since they seem to have had no contacts in the city, and their spoken Italian was not yet fluent but they may have seen the journal. *Il Conciliatore* admired Salvatore Viganò, a great dancer and choreographer whose ballets such as *Prometeo* and *Giovanna d'Arco* expressed his revolutionary ideas. At Milan's subsidised theatre, La Scala, Viganò was able to combine his genius for choreography with scenery, music and costumes of an equally high standard to create a magnificent artistic experience, whereas the commercial English theatre had to put making money before artistic excellence. Shelley's response to Viganò's work was profound. Italy, Italian history and art, were to inspire Shelley over the next four years. From Milan, they went to Livorno to meet John and Maria Gisborne. Maria, a friend of Godwin's, had looked after Mary as a baby.

It is always a difficult thing to leave one's own country and attempt to settle in another. Shelley was 25 and although he and Mary had wanted to go to Italy, he was homesick. His sense of exile expressed itself at first in very unpleasant xenophobic remarks about the Italian people, complaining for instance that they ate garlic! This attitude towards people he had come to live amongst was unworthy of Shelley, as he dressed up prejudice as political comment. In describing the beauty of Venice to Peacock, he added 'Venice which was once a tyrant, is now the next worse thing, a slave'.[5] This attitude did not last and he came to love both the country and its inhabitants.

As Italy had so recently suffered revolution, invasion, occupation, and restoration, Italians were exhausted politically. This was something which many visitors from England, including the Shelleys, did not fully understand. Coming from a country where there were riots, uprisings and reform agitation, it seemed to them that Italians were not sufficiently politically active, particularly as the English recognised that the Italians were suffering greater oppression. The movements which would result within 40 years in a united Italy, independent of the Austrian and Bourbons were then nascent. For some liberals and 'Jacobins' that would not have been the goal, republicanism being more important. It was probably Byron, who had become part of Venetian society, who helped Shelley to appreciate the Italian efforts to become independent.

Shelley never became as involved in Italian politics as Byron but he did not entirely leave his political heart in England and his knowledge of Italian affairs broadened his international view. He kept in touch with events in England by arranging to have *The Examiner* and Cobbett's *Political Register* sent to him. Cobbett had fled to America after the suspension of Habeas Corpus in 1817 but felt quite able to comment on English affairs and to continue to edit his *Register* from there. Peacock may also have sent Shelley *The Black Dwarf*, as he appears to have known in detail about events concerning Henry

Hunt and the reformers which were discussed in that paper. Peacock sent him other papers and wrote political news himself, for example, concerning the 1818 elections.[6]

Although one of the reasons for travelling to Italy was to take Allegra to her father, now living in Venice, Shelley did his best to assure Claire that she need not part with her child, but Claire thought she was doing her best for Allegra. Byron refused to see Claire at all and she suffered greatly when Allegra was sent to Venice in April 1818 with the nursemaid, Elise. Shelley agreed to take Claire to Venice in August to see if Byron would allow her to spend some time with Allegra. Byron was amenable, and offered the Shelleys the use of a country villa he rented. Shelley urgently sent for Mary and the children but the urgency was not, as some have supposed, to conceal her absence from Byron since Shelley informed him of her arrival a week later on 13 September.[7] However, the haste had a terrible consequence. One-year-old Clara had been ill with a fever and, although she seems to have recovered in time to make the journey, it fatigued her and she had a relapse. Her parents took her to Venice to see a specialist but the poor baby died before they even got there. Mary suffered what Shelley called 'a kind of despair' which probably would now be described as 'clinical depression'.[8] They visited Byron in Venice, and Shelley began his revolutionary 'lyric drama' *Prometheus Unbound* and the *Lines Written Among the Euganean Hills* at the villa.

Naples

The Shelleys lived for the winter in a smart part of the city of Naples but were unable to afford to go often to the opera, though they did climb Vesuvius and they saw the excavated remains at Pompeii and Herculaneum. These journeys would inspire Shelley's imagery associated with volcanoes in *Prometheus Unbound*, 'the city disinterred' in his *Ode to Naples* (1, PW, p. 616), and 'old palaces and towers' under the ocean in the *Ode to the West Wind* (33). The Neapolitan clergy and aristocracy had opposed the Napoleonic reforms and the peasantry associated 'Jacobinism' with high taxation, conscription and despoliation of their churches but Murat had won a measure of loyalty among the middle class as he had shown some independence from French rule. He was executed by the returning Bourbons. There was widespread resentment and in trying to placate all parties, the king's minister failed. Because of two bloody counter-revolutions, there were many who had joined the brigands, and the roads were dangerous for travellers as Shelley found while travelling south.[9]

Claire thought in 1875–76 that Shelley had been one of the Carbonari, a secret society, usually consisting of army officers and small bourgeoisie. Claire's later beliefs and stories about Shelley are not always reliable. She said that Byron 'hated Shelley' and 'despised his poetry and his principles', although Byron's respect for Shelley's poetry and defence of his character to Thomas Moore and others suggests the reverse.[10] Despite the fact that Shelley was against secret societies, he may have been sympathetic if the Neapolitan Carbonari included revolutionaries influenced by French ideals and in Italy the 'Jacobins' were influenced by Filippo Buonarotti, one of Babeuf's 'Conspiracy of Equals'.[11] Shelley doubtless knew Carbonari in Naples, but it is unlikely that he actually signed up, since his useful skills, such as being a good rider and a good shot, would be outweighed by his poor health. He was undergoing medical treatment which was probably causing him more health problems than any disease. Naples was warm and sea bathing was recommended for many complaints.[12] Shelley was also very depressed. One of the causes may have been a blackmail attempt which Shelley referred to as 'taking advantage of my situation in Naples'. This has been understood to refer to a story that Shelley and Claire had a child. Shelley did give his name to a little girl, Elena, born in December 1818 but the mother is unknown. As the number of abandoned children since the war had grown by 70 per cent in Florence, five-fold in Milan and probably similarly in Naples, it is possible that Shelley came across such a child and wanted to adopt her.[13] He made arrangements for Elena to be cared for while an infant by foster-parents and then for her to join Mary and himself, but Elena sadly died of a fever before he could collect her.

Rome

The Shelleys went on to Rome, where Shelley continued *Prometheus Unbound*, the story of a successful and (almost) non-violent revolution. In *Prometheus Bound* by the classical Greek poet Aeschylus, Prometheus, the Titan, was punished by Zeus for giving fire to humans. Prometheus was suspended on a mountainside with an eagle eating his liver. In the lost sequel by Aeschylus, Prometheus and Zeus were reconciled, but Shelley said that he did not want the resolution of the drama to be one 'so feeble as that of reconciling the Champion with the Oppressor' (p. 229). Shelley's Prometheus does not become reconciled with Jupiter (Shelley used the Latin names for the Graeco-Roman gods) but he does repent that he cursed him, saying 'I wish no living thing to suffer pain' (I, i, 305). At his repentance, extraordinary things begin to happen. He is able to communicate, though at second-hand and through a dream experienced by her sister, with his wife, Asia, who symbolises Love as he symbolises Mind (or intelligence). Asia and her sister are led on a journey to the centre of the earth where she meets Demogorgon, a dark, veiled, shapeless figure, who responds to her questions in a riddling way, but who tells her that 'all things are subject to' 'Fate, Time, Occasion, Chance and Change' but 'eternal Love' (III, iv, 119/120). Asia asks when Prometheus will 'arise/Henceforth the Sun of this rejoicing world' and Demogorgon responds 'Behold' (III, iv, 127–8). A charioteer takes Asia to join the now liberated Prometheus. Demogorgon in another chariot arrives to remove Jupiter, tells Jupiter he is 'Eternity' and takes him down into 'the wide waves of ruin' (III, i, 71). Jupiter's fall is violent, although he does not fall alone but with Demogorgon. Both Demogorgon and Jupiter are cast into Eternity, although Demogorgon reappears at the end of Act IV to advise what action to take to prevent Jupiter rising again. Too close a correspondence between the allegorical figures and agents of change in political life is unwise, but Demogorgon has been held to be the 'People Monster'.[14] It is perhaps through the action of the people, combining love and intelligence, that both tyranny and oppression will disappear into eternity. In April, Shelley completed three acts of the drama, with Jupiter's fall. He continued to add scenes and songs to the earlier acts until December 1819 and a fourth act which extended the rejoicing at the liberation of humanity.[15]

Shelley has been accused of not writing in a 'popular' style and therefore not for working people, a criticism particularly levelled at *Prometheus Unbound*. The implication is that working people can only appreciate very simple poetry and artists should deliberately avoid experiment. This is a narrow view, held by Stalin. Revolution-ary artists can also be innovators in art – as Picasso and the artists of the Russian Revolution were initially – and the audience comes to appreciate their work. Shelley wrote *Prometheus*, his 'favourite' poem, for 'select classes of poetical readers' in an experimental 'best style', a 'drama with characters and mechanisms of a kind yet unattempted'.[16] He did not think that upper-class people had better taste, as he believed that 'the vulgarity of rank and fashion is as gross in its way as that of poverty'.[17] Viganò's popular ballets and Aeschylus' tragedies, which influenced *Prometheus*, were, although the highest art, written for mass audiences. *Prometheus* inspired William Benbow, who intended to publish it in 1826 'for the humble in place and purse'.[18] Gisborne thought that it had had a wider circulation than Shelley was aware of, as the Tory *Quarterly Review* had given it a lengthy review, which they would not have done unless the work was likely to be read. Shelley attached importance to reading poetry aloud, a pastime which the Shelleys often enjoyed in the evening, as many others did in the nineteenth century, and he believed that Gisborne would have been a better person than the scholarly Peacock to see *Prometheus Unbound* through the press, as Gisborne had 'heard it recited, and will therefore more readily seize any error'.[19] Shelley translated Plato's *Symposium* so that people, including women, with no knowledge of Greek could have access to Plato's ideas. Had he been elitist, he would not have bothered to do this.

The Cenci

The Shelleys loved Rome. They did not want to meet any English people, Shelley saying, 'the manners of the rich English are something wholly insupportable'. They met Italians at the house of Mariana Dionigi and now Shelley was able to say that 'the Romans please me much, especially the women'.[20] Their Roman friends discussed the story of Beatrice Cenci, a young woman in the sixteenth century who had murdered her father, Count Cenci, a murderer who ill-treated his children and his wife and who raped Beatrice. They discussed whether the murder was justified in the circumstances: the historical Beatrice had claimed that it was not parricide since Cenci had forfeited his right to be considered her father. Shelley, who had already seen a manuscript version of the story belonging to John Gisborne, was prompted to write his historical tragedy *The Cenci* (pp. 315–17).

Selflessly courageous and loving, Beatrice refuses to leave home and abandon her brother and stepmother, who patiently suffers her husband's abuse for the sake of her stepchildren. She defies her father and the Church. Orsino, a priest attracted to Beatrice, has seen that her petitions to the Pope do not reach him. The Pope has already agreed to 'hush up' a murder Cenci has committed in return for a third of his estate, something announced in the very first line of the play. Beatrice's choice is between suffering his attacks or committing murder, but immediately after the murder, the Pope's legates come to arrest Cenci for his earlier crimes. The Pope, i.e. the State, has the right to commit legal murder, but Shelley believed no one had that right. Although Beatrice has his sympathy which he expects his audience or reader to share, he shows that her action contaminates her but when she faces death calmly she reveals her ultimate nobility of character. Shelley believed that committing a violent act changed people including those who take part in a violent revolution.

Although very heavily censored, theatre was the most popular form of entertainment in Regency England, attended by people from all classes. Shelley sent *The Cenci* to the Theatre Royal, Covent Garden. He wanted their fine actress, Eliza O'Neill, to play Beatrice.[21] But he was unlucky. O'Neill had just retired, and the theatre manager thought that the incest in the play, even though not directly mentioned, would prevent it being performed. The Theatre Royal, Drury Lane, also turned it down.[22] *The Cenci* was not performed professionally in England until 1922, when another great actress, Sybil Thorndike, played Beatrice. It was – and is – generally agreed to be the finest tragedy of the period.

Shelley undoubtedly wished the question of violence against women to be discussed since he had raised it in an earlier poem, *Rosalind and Helen*, but he was thinking of a broader application of the theme to politics. He dates his dedication to Leigh Hunt 'May 29, 1819' (p. 314), but he did not complete the play until August, so he chose the date to commemorate the 'enmity with domestic and political tyranny and imposture' which he and Hunt shared. It is the anniversary of Charles II's restoration, Oak Apple Day, celebrated in Georgian England with conker-style games with acorns, and beating those not wearing oak leaves with stinging nettles.[23] Although the games and rituals were doubtless rooted in the same folk traditions as the bonfires and maypoles which Shelley enjoyed, he would have detested their being made to serve ultra-royalist propaganda and the date is a reference to the Regency tyranny. When *The Cenci* was published it was popular enough for Henry 'Orator' Hunt to be unable to get a copy so it clearly reached a wide and radical audience.[24]

Writing two masterpieces over the same period was even more of an achievement considering that Shelley was grieving deeply for two beloved children. The Shelleys' son, William, who was three and a half, died. Shelley sat by his bedside for '60, miserable, deathlyke hours' and said that he felt as if he 'should never recover any cheerfulness again'.[25] Mary, who was pregnant, became deeply depressed. This wasn't helped by a series of amazingly unsympathetic letters from her father as a result of which Shelley decided to keep correspondence away from her. In a fragmentary verse, Shelley expressed his feelings that she had 'gone / And left me in this dreary world alone', but that he could not follow her to 'Sorrow's most obscure abo[de]' for her own sake'.[26] The plan had been to return to Naples, but after William's death they moved to Livorno to be near the Gisbornes. Shelley found that working on *The Cenci* 'was a fine antidote to nervous medicines' and exacerbated the pain in his side. This was the only work he discussed with Mary, so he may have tried to help bring her out of her depression by doing so.[27]

Peterloo

The year 1819 has been called Shelley's *Annus Mirabilis*. *Julian and Maddalo*, among his longer poems, is a dialogue or 'conversation' poem which draws on a ride he took with Byron in Venice, in which Julian argues for a positive view of human nature and destiny as opposed to the more pessimistic Maddalo. Shelley also wrote shorter poems, but when he received the news of the 'Peterloo Massacre' he became even more prolific.

Shelley would have known about the 1818 Manchester cotton spinners' strike, since Cobbett's *Register* for 10 December 1818 was an open letter of congratulation to them on their action. Their union was 'quasi-legal' and although they supported reform they were not leaders among the reform movement for fear of blacklisting. Weavers, too, had struck throughout Manchester, Bolton, Burnley and Bury during 1818. Henry Hunt presented a further petition to the Prince Regent which was rejected. The split in the reform movement was shown in Westminster at the 1818 election and the 1819 by-election. Cobbett and Hunt had succeeded in discrediting Burdett, characterising him as the 'fox-hunting baronet', although they themselves were property owners and farmers, not agricultural or industrial workers. Yet Jeremy Bentham had converted Burdett to universal suffrage and had become influential with the Westminster Committee, whose preferred candidates were Henry Brougham and John Cam Hobhouse, Byron's friend. Cartwright, who deserved credit for his lifelong devotion to reform and his leadership in forming Hampden clubs also stood but Cobbett no longer supported Hampden Clubs. Cobbett supported Hunt's campaign while *Sherwin's Political Register* published his campaign material, but Hunt did not support Cobbett when he suggested flooding the country with forged banknotes, something Shelley described as 'very comic'.[28] The Tory George Lamb was elected. Shelley commented to Peacock in May 1819, 'I saw the lst numbers were Lamb 4200 & Hobhouse 3900 14th day. There is little hope. That mischievous Cobbet has divided & weakened the interest of the popular party so that the factions who prey upon our country, have been able to coalesce to its exclusion'.[29] This was indeed what had happened although this was not clear to many at the time. On 24 August, Shelley wrote, 'England seems to be in a very disturbed state', but he did not know until September about what had occurred at Manchester's St Peter's Fields on 16 August.[30]

Henry Hunt wanted to proceed in a legal and constitutional way for 'Universal Suffrage and Annual Parliaments, and an opposition to all laws that have a tendency to curtail the Liberties of the People, and oppress and starve the Poor', but he did not want 'an equal division of property' or 'no poor people'. Hunt wished that 'the man, poor and industrious, who laboured from one end of the week to the other, should have something more than the necessaries of life [. . .] something against a wet day'. Workers were forming groups and collecting funds as steps towards founding a 'national union' all over the country, particularly in the northwest of England. In January 1819, Hunt had spoken at a meeting of between 8,000 and 10,000 in St Peter's Fields, Manchester, with so many on the platform that it collapsed. In Birmingham, the reformer Sir Charles Wolseley was elected as an alternative representative to Parliament. This was illegal and was also threatening: Sinn Fein used the tactic of an alternative parliament in 1919, exactly one hundred years later. The authorities were alarmed, and the Manchester magistrates contacted the Home Secretary, Sidmouth, when a meeting for 9 August was proposed for this purpose at St Peter's Fields. They declared the meeting illegal, so the organisers proposed a meeting for 16 August, 'to consider the propriety of adopting the most legal means of obtaining a Reform in the commons house of Parliament'. As Hunt had heard there was a warrant for his arrest, he went to the magistrates to offer himself up. They said they had no warrant. In other words, the meeting which took place was perfectly legal.[31]

Numerous eyewitnesses reported the orderly arrival of delegations at St Peter's Fields on 16 August 1819, 'in their Sunday clothes, wives and children included, unarmed and cheerful', carrying silk banners inscribed 'Unity and Strength', 'Parliaments, Annual', 'Suffrage, Universal'. Hunt had requested 'quietness and order' and the contingents had even left their walking sticks at a house along the way to avoid being accused of carrying weapons.[32] Hunt, in his white top hat, arrived and took his place on the rostrum. Nearby were women and children, flags and music. Suddenly, yeomanry, drawn from local employers, followed by soldiers, rode into the crowd, striking with their sabres. For a time the crowd gave way and allowed them to arrest Hunt, but when they began to panic the yeomanry charged, killing eleven people and injuring hundreds of others, either by wounds or by being trampled by the horses.[33]

As E.P. Thompson observed, 'it really was a bloody massacre'. The yeomanry vented their class hatred on the crowd, some of whom they knew, making remarks such as 'There's Saxton, damn him' and 'Damn you, what mean you by this work?'[34] The culpability of the authorities in sending armed troops on horseback to attack a completely peaceful crowd is clear. Within two days, Carlile in *Sherwin's Political Register* and John Tyas in *The Times* had published eyewitness reports. Shelley replied to Peacock on 9 September, thanking him for 'sending the papers' with the news of Manchester and on the 21st he repeated, 'I have received all the papers you sent me, & the Examiners'. Peacock therefore probably sent him all the papers he could on the subject.[35]

Shelley replied with the most famous political protest poem in English, *The Mask of Anarchy*, which he sent to *The Examiner* on 23 September. Its image of the ruling class riding through the people of Britain, anarchic in the sense of being totally disordered and thus reflecting the way in which they ruled England, comes from the description of the bloody yeomen rampaging through the orderly Manchester crowd; an image of physical slaughter but also, meta-phorically, of the dreadful destruction of people's lives wreaked by the ruling class every day and the murder of human rights. The rulers are Fraud, Murder and Hypocrisy; easy enough to characterise in Regency England where Sidmouth had given the go ahead to shed blood at Manchester but wanted to build new churches, where Castlereagh had played a part in the savage suppression of the 1798 rising in Ireland, where Lord Eldon had pushed through the 1795 Sedition Acts and opposed the abolition of the slave trade. They all participated in the fraud, murder and hypocrisy and all of them worshipped 'GOD, AND KING, AND LAW' (37). Their ghastly king-like symbol is Anarchy, a skeleton figure perhaps inspired by the caricature *The Masquerade* by Thomas Rowlandson in *The English Dance of Death* (1815–16).[36]

The meeting at Manchester symbolised the hope of the people and in the poem Hope, who 'looked more like Despair' (l. 88) runs in front of the cavalcade to sacrifice herself. Out of hope something else is created, something that kills Anarchy and his murderous allies. Once again, as in *Prometheus*, the oppressors are destroyed by something intangible: Hope's sacrifice has caused a different mood to arise, a 'sense awakening' (136), a determination brought about by the realisation of the wrongs which the oppressed had suffered. They are now expressed and from their expression strength grows. Shelley then turned from symbolism to the next step. 'Let a great Assembly be' (262), one which will not include just the Manchester region but the whole country and everyone in it, young old, sick or healthy, even some 'from the palaces' (283) where, as Shelley knew, there were people who felt 'such compassion' (298). This assembly should then declare that they were free and allow the tyrants to charge them. The result would be that the attackers would be ashamed, and that the slaughter will steam up like inspiration, 'eloquent, oracular' (362). Oppression's thundered doom' (365) will be the words 'Rise like lions after slumber' (368).

But at Manchester, as Shelley knew, the meeting had been peaceful and the yeomanry who had attacked it were indeed scorned by the whole country. The crowd did not stand firm when charged, although they may have done so at first. It would have been a physical impossibility to expect the mother of two-year-old William Fildes, who was thrown out of her arms and trampled upon, to react calmly. This advice is not a metaphor since Shelley offers it once again in *A Philosophical View of Reform*. He believed that a revolution would be achieved through a willingness to passively resist a charge of the kind. He was not alone in this. Samuel Bamford discussed radical politics with soldiers and soldiers were to support Queen Caroline in 1820. Many radical journalists believed that it would be possible for the demonstrators to win over the soldiers. This has happened in a revolutionary situation, as with the Cossacks in the 1917 Russian Revolution. The French soldiers in 1789 who refused to fire on the crowd at Versailles might well have been in Shelley's mind.[37] In *A Philosophical View*, Shelley suggests that the soldier's instinct to chase after a fleeing crowd is the reason for standing firm. Soldiers would be deterred by 'an unresisting multitude bearing in their looks the calm deliberate resolution to perish rather than not assert their rights' (p. 669). But the Manchester yeomanry were from the employer class, not brothers or professional soldiers; Shelley knew this because he calls them 'the tyrants'. His idea is to peacefully face the enemy, consistent with Quakerism.

The Mask of Anarchy was not published until 1832, after the Reform Bill had been passed, but then it became overwhelmingly popular and has remained a part of the heritage of the working class. Its most quoted lines are the final verse, which also appear earlier in the poem:

> Rise like lions after slumber
> In unvanquishable number
> Shake your chains to earth like dew
> Which in sleep had fallen on you –
> Ye are many – they are few.

Though Shelley himself referred to 'the many and the few' in *Queen Mab*, Henry Hunt would also repeat, 'We are many, they are few' in his speeches. Shelley changed it to 'Ye' as the words are spoken by the spirit of Liberty.[38]

If the poem had been published at the time it would have been immediately popular and inspiring. The mood in the country in the two months following Peterloo was very much that of lions. Newspapers were carrying angry articles – the *Medusa* wanted 'the blowing up of the present system' and stated 'everywhere summary justice is required'. Hone, who believed that after Peterloo there was no alternative to revolution, produced his witty parodies *The Political House that Jack Built* and *The Man in the Moon* with cartoons by George Cruikshank. 'There is scarcely a street or a post in the land but that it is placarded with something seditious.'[39] Burdett wrote his constituents an angry open letter which landed him in jail with a £2,000 fine. The Spenceans organised a mass meeting at Smithfield on 29 August. In these circumstances, it would have been possible to unite the Reformers against the government and oblige it to concede demands, perhaps even universal suffrage. Shelley was to suggest this in *A Philosophical View of Reform*.[40]

A Philosophical View of Reform

It was agreed that Henry Hunt had behaved very well at Peterloo. The Spenceans and the Westminster Committee arranged a triumphal entry into London on 13 September when 300,000 people, including the poet Keats, lined the streets, followed by a dinner in Hunt's honour.[41] He managed to alienate them by demanding to take the chair instead of Gale Jones and leaving Watson, who three months later was imprisoned for its non-payment, with the bill. Nevertheless, Hunt was still the hero of Peterloo and very influential. So when he insisted on a 'constitutional' and 'legal' approach, the various 'Political Protestant' societies followed his advice. Instead of taking direct action, the energy went into unsuccessful law suits against the yeomanry of Peterloo, unrealised hopes of obtaining a Parliamentary enquiry and in getting funds for Hunt's own defence, although he lost the trial. Whigs, radicals and Spenceans, and even the Lord Lieutenant of Yorkshire organised protest meetings. 'Meetings [. . .] throughout the Kingdom on one and the same day' were proposed for 1 November, which would have amounted to a general strike, the equivalent of the 'great assembly' suggested by Shelley. It was taken up in Manchester, Huddersfield, Newcastle and many other northern towns. Hunt denounced the plan and Thistlewood, one of the Spencean leaders, as a spy. It has been suggested that Thistlewood took part in the 1820 Cato Street Conspiracy (to assassinate members of the Cabinet) to prove Hunt wrong over his accusation.[42]

Henry Hunt believed that the solution to all problems was universal suffrage, annual parliaments and a secret ballot. He was a great fighter, consistent in his approach all his life, but he refused to see any other point of view and quarrelled with the other reformers, whom he viciously denounced. With a vision no larger than reforming the voting system, he betrayed the working people who supported him. By December 1819 it was impossible to organise meetings as the government passed the 'Six Acts' which were even more stringent than the Seditious Meetings Act already in force: public meetings, particularly mass meetings of more than 50 to be held out of doors, were banned, meeting places had to be licensed by JPs, political pamphlets subject to taxation, magistrates were empowered to search for arms, drilling was to become illegal.[43]

In October 1819, Shelley had written again to Leigh Hunt asking about *The Mask of Anarchy* and in December sent him a letter defending Richard Carlile who was to be tried for publishing Paine's works. 'For what was Mr. Carlile prosecuted? For impugning the Divinity of Jesus Christ? I impugn it. For denying that the whole mass of antient Hebrew literature is of divine authority? I deny it'. Shelley points out that a jury of Christians would condemn Paine, a Deist, whereas a jury of Deists would be likely to acquit him: 'deism' is 'no crime'. 'Aristocratical' deists are not prosecuted; Carlile is because he is a 'starving bookseller'. The state is 'crushing a political enemy'. He suggests a subscription for Carlile.[44] Shelley himself was out of danger of prosecution being in Italy, but he had run the same risk as Carlile with *The Necessity of Atheism*, and probably realised that his social status and minority had protected him. Shelley was 'considerably interested' in this letter but Leigh Hunt did not publish it, although he did publish others in Carlile's defence. It is a pity that Carlile never knew of Shelley's support or that Leigh Hunt never passed Shelley's work on to Carlile, who admired Shelley. Carlile had published Shelley's *Declaration of Rights* in *The Republican* of 24 September 1819 followed by comments similar to those Shelley expresses in *A Philosophical View of Reform*.[45] Carlile may not have known who wrote the *Declaration* and Shelley may never have seen *The Republican*.

By ignoring these major works but publishing Shelley's much slighter *Love's Philosophy*, Leigh Hunt sent Shelley a message that he recognised that Shelley wanted to go further than Hunt, as editor, was willing to go in his anti-government stance. Shelley then asked Ollier about publishing 'an octavo on reform – a commonplace kind of book [. . .] an instructive and readable book, appealing from the passions to the reason of men'. When no reply came from Ollier, he asked Leigh Hunt if he knew

> any bookseller who wd. publish for me an octavo volume entitled 'A Philosophical View of Reform'. It is boldly but temperately written - & I think readable – It is intended for a kind of standard book for the philosophical reformers politically considered, like Jeremy Bentham's something, [*Plan of Parliamentary Reform in the Form of a Catechism*] but different & perhaps more systematic.[46]

Once again, no reply. He offered it to the Olliers again in July 1820, saying he felt obliged to offer them the work first since they were his publishers.[47] Hone or Carlile would probably have published it, but if Shelley had wanted them to do so, he could not know if they were still publishing or if they were in jail. He needed someone in England to act as his agent, as Peacock had done in taking *The Cenci* to the theatres. Probably this lack of response caused Shelley to abandon both the 'volume of popular songs' he was proposing and *A Philosophical View of Reform*, which was not published until 1920.[48]

On 23 January 1819, Shelley had written to Peacock,

> I consider Poetry very subordinate to moral & political science, & if I were well, certainly I should aspire to the latter; for I can conceive a great work, embodying the discoveries of all ages, & harmonizing the contending creeds by which mankind have been ruled. Far from me is such an attempt & I shall be content by exercising my fancy to amuse myself & perhaps some others, & cast what weight I can into the right scale of that balance which the Giant (of Arthegal) holds.[49]

Peacock noted that Shelley was alluding to the Giant in Spenser's poem, *The Faerie Queene*:

> The Giant has scales, in which he professes to weigh right and wrong, and rectify the physical and moral evils, which result from inequality of condition. Shelley once pointed out this passage to me, observing: 'Artegall argues with the Giant; the Giant has the best of the argument; Artegall's iron man knocks him over into the sea and drowns him. This is the usual way in which power deals with opinion.' I said: 'That was not the lesson which Spenser intended to convey.' 'Perhaps not,' he said; 'it is the lesson which he conveys to me. I am of the Giant's faction'.[50]

A Philosophical View is not the work Shelley mentioned to Peacock, nor does he make any concessions to Bentham; in fact Shelley's views on the national debt and 'paper money', were closer to Cobbett and on distribution of wealth to Spence and Babeuf. *A Philosophical View* does not merely discuss the question of reform of Parliament as might be inferred from the description he offers Ollier and Leigh Hunt. It goes much further, and here Peacock's gloss on Shelley's attitude towards power is helpful. At the time when the people of England were being suppressed, Shelley was attempting a reply on behalf of the Giant who is on the side of equality. His first chapter provides a historical overview of class struggle from the Roman

Empire ('that vast and successful scheme for the enslaving of the most civilised portion of mankind', p. 637). He shows that there has always been a struggle against tyranny, in the Italian Republics, the Reformation and the establishment of the Dutch Republic, the English Revolution and the justice meted to 'one of those chiefs of a conspiracy of privileged murderers and robbers' (Charles I). He concludes that 'the principles of human nature as applied to men in political society' are the 'rules of freedom and equality [. . .] according to which the happiness resulting from the social union ought to be produced and distributed'. (p. 639) Yet despite great technical and commercial progress, brought about by the English Revolution, this had not been achieved in his native country.

In 1819, there was no need for the arguments of *Putting Reform to the Vote* – Shelley believed that there was 'an almost universal sentiment' that change is necessary. The 'manufacturers [factory workers] to a man' wanted reform and 'an immense majority of the inhabitants of London' (p. 670). 'Those interested in maintaining the contrary' ('I mean the government party') say that it can only come about by violence (p. 647). Shelley implies that 'temporary popular violence' could not be worse than 'the mischiefs of permanent tyrannical and fraudulent forms of government'. It is a choice between 'despotism and anarchy' (pp. 647–8).

It is necessary because of the disproportionate inequality of the distribution of wealth. 'The majority of the people' are 'ill-clothed, ill-fed and ill-educated', but not so much so that they do not 'know this' (p. 655). Their labour produces the wealth since all property is the produce of labour. They are robbed of their natural rights by the national debt, introduced to pay for 'two liberticide wars' against France and America, and 'paper money' (p. 657); the money owed could have been used to improve the conditions of working people, with better education, housing and clothes – 'a paradise of comfort' with 'a nice collection of useful books'. This is not a utopian future; he is explaining what the present could have been like. He saw that working people were deprived of education and resented it. Their great thirst for education was shown when mechanics' institutes and libraries were established over the next few decades. In 1815, the interest on the public debt was £37,500,000 and the rate of exchange unfavourable because of excessive use of paper money.[51]

Shelley followed Cobbett in believing that, since the bank could never pay the money in gold, the 'paper money' issue was fraudulent and more crucial to the economic problem than it was but he does not put the weight on it that Cobbett does. Shelley could not have been uninformed about the stock exchange as he would undoubtedly have discussed it with his friend, Horace Smith. For him, the problem is far deeper, namely a class war which has worsened since the aristocracy of land was joined by the aristocracy of 'stock jobbers, usurers, directors, government pensions, country bankers: a set of pelting wretches who think of any commerce with their species as a means not an end', although the chivalric ideal of the aristocracy 'at the bottom [. . .] is all trick' (p.652). The 'hereditary aristocracy' 'created this other' (p. 653) which has forced poor people to work 16 hours instead of eight, even the sick and elderly, and turned children into machines who should be playing in front of their cottage door (p. 651). This view of early industrial society is expressed in language similar to Owen's. What is more, Malthusians want to deprive the poor of the right to have children: a right they do not deny the rich (p. 655). The people should be 'instructed in the whole truth' and know their rights.[52]

Shelley's reform programme is similar to Cobbett's: abolish the national debt, the standing army, sinecures and tithes, make all religions and non-religion legally equal and make justice cheap, certain and speedy (p. 655). Shelley believed that a government elected to do this should oblige the rich to pay the national debt as it is a 'debt contracted by the privileged classes towards one portion of themselves' but 'the interest is chiefly paid by those who had no hand in the borrowing' (p. 661). Some who are termed 'property owners' are not much better off than the labouring classes – 'I mean not every man who possesses any degree of property; I mean the rich' (p. 659). Artisans, farmers, mechanics, doctors, artists and writers work for their living and should be allowed to leave something to their children, but not the aristocracy, who got their money by 'usurpation, imposture, violence' and don't deserve it (p. 660). On this basis,

Shelley was saying that he deserved to keep anything he earned with his pen, but not his family estate.

If there was any chance that reform would come via Parliament, Shelley wanted to take it as he felt that a concession would prevent an insurrection, something he does not want, not because he wants the situation to continue as it is but because he feels that the resulting chaos would re-establish a tyranny, as it did after the English and French Revolutions. There were three reform possibilities.

1. Reform could come from the existing Parliament, which could begin by disenfranchising the rotten boroughs and transferring the seats to the unrepresented cities. Shelley felt it would be best to accept this, then press for more 'with firmness and moderation'. Thus people would become 'habituated' to 'exercising the functions of sovereignty'.
2. A government more open to reform could be elected. If so, Shelley would vote for a property qualification and triennial parliaments. Given contemporary prejudice against women, the vote for women is 'somewhat immature', although he is himself in favour of it, but he does not like the impersonality of voting by secret ballot since it does not give an opportunity for 'the elector and the elected' to 'understand each other' (p. 665).
3. If 'the Houses of Parliament obstinately and perpetually refuse to concede any reform' Shelley's vote would be for the universal suffrage, equal representation and annual parliaments demanded by the radical reformers even though he describes these measures as 'ill-digested systems of democracy' (p. 667). To Shelley they fell short of the 1793 French Constitution, which, among other things enshrined the rights of free exercise of religion, liberty of the press, petition and to hold public assemblies, and far short of Babeuf's demands or Shelley's own *Declaration of Rights*.[53] Why do the reformers not demand 'the immediate abolition of [. . .] monarchy and aristocracy, and the levelling of inordinate wealth, and an agrarian distribution, including the Parks and Chases of the rich, of the uncultivated districts of the country' (p. 662), a suggestion similar to that expressed in Spence's *The Constitution of a Perfect Commonwealth*. Universal suffrage might bring these

about, but in that case it would 'produce an immature attempt at a republic. It is better that [an] object so inexpressibly great and sacred should never have been attempted than that it should be attempted and fail' (p. 662).

Shelley was right to believe that for 'Commons [to] reform itself, uninfluenced by any fear that the people would, on their refusal, assume to itself that office seems a contradiction' (p. 663). Although a Parliamentary inquiry was set up in 1819 into electoral practice in Grampound, Cornwall, in 1821 the seats were not transferred to the cities which needed them but to the huge county of Yorkshire which didn't.[54]

So how was a reform to be gained? The government 'possess [. . .] a standing army and [. . .] a legion of spies and police officers' (p. 677).

They would disperse any assembly really chosen by the people; they would shoot and hew down any multitude without regard to sex or age [. . .] which might be collected in its defence; they would calumniate, imprison, starve, ruin, and expatriate every person who wrote or acted, or thought, or might be suspected to think against them; misery and extermination would fill the country from one end to another . . . (p. 667)

On the other hand, action should be taken immediately, otherwise 'this condition of things' will become 'as permanent as the system of castes in India' (p. 667). Shelley believed that the 'few who aspire to' more than reform should 'wait until a modified advantage is obtained' and then press for other demands. Meanwhile, these 'true patriot[s]' should enlighten and unite the nation, spread 'political truth' and confidence and enthusiasm, appealing to what 'the divided friends of liberty [. . .] are all agreed on' but by publishing treatises, petitions, mass meetings and refusing taxes (p. 668).

'All might, however, be ineffectual' (p. 669). Mary Shelley had said that 'a revolution [. . .] would [not?] be <u>bloodless</u> if [Cobbett] has any power in it', so presumably the Shelleys hoped for a 'bloodless' revolution.[55] This must have been relative, however, since Shelley did not think that there would be no struggle. He had already warned that 'so dear is power that the tyrants themselves neither then nor now nor ever left or leave a path to freedom but through their own blood' (p. 638) and remarked that in the French Revolution 'the tyrants were as usual, the aggressors' although 'the oppressed [. . .] took a dreadful revenge' (p. 644). Shelley was concerned with the dangers of counter-revolution and with the hazard that militarisation would pose to a revolution by enabling a new tyranny. War is inevitably linked to tyranny, and 'demagogues, oligarchies and usurpers are merely varieties of the same class' (p. 673). 'The true friend of mankind [. . .] would hesitate before he recommended measures which tend to bring down so heavy a calamity as civil war, but it seemed that 'the madness of parties admits no other mode of determining the question at issue' (p. 673). As in his poems, Shelley left out exactly how the people were going to win, but he assumed that 'the people shall have obtained, by whatever means, the victory over their oppressors'. In that case, he warned against revenge (p. 674).

Some of the activities Shelley advised were being carried on. Cobbett, Carlile, Hone, Wooler and others were publishing 'the truth'. Carlile and his wife, family, friends and volunteers continued to publish and spent a total of 200 years in prison.[56] Public pressure got Carlile released in 1825. Shelley advised the reformers not to wait. Although he said, 'It is better that we gain what we demand by a process of negotiation which would occupy twenty years' than to risk civil war, which he knew that the ruling class would inflict, 'the last resort of resistance is undoubtedly insurrection [. . .] derived from the employment of armed force to counteract the will of the nation' (p. 672). Shelley thought the use of violence was justified because of the injustices perpetrated by the ruling class: 'a successful conspiracy to defraud and oppress' (p. 667).

Shelley hoped his treatise would influence the Benthamites as he wanted all the reformers to unite. Bentham's views were popular among trades clubs, especially shoemakers, and had a Parliamentary link through Burdett. However, Shelley had not much faith in the leadership of Cobbett and Henry Hunt – rightly, since Hunt's delays and damping down of the enthusiasm of his supporters meant that the impetus was lost. Possibly, Shelley hoped the leadership would pass from the 'demagogues' to new leaders from the groups recently formed in northern towns, the 'few who aspire to more' (p. 654) than the reform of Parliament. Hunt's leadership was too strong for this to happen, although not strong enough to lead to victory. He lost leadership of the reform movement to the Whigs. Reform agitation did not revive until Daniel O'Connell's movement in Ireland forced the Tory government to grant Catholic Emancipation. The divided Tories allowed the Whigs to get in, and the Whigs proceeded with the Reform Act which gave the vote to more property owners.

Shelley would not have expected to wait so long for such a feeble reform as the 1832 Reform Act turned out to be. He certainly would not have expected to wait until 1928 for a simple democratic measure like universal suffrage, which was first demanded in the 1780s. When he mentioned 20 years, it seemed a long time to him; he was, at the time, only 27. For Shelley, getting the vote was only a part of democracy and enlarging the franchise only a strategy to gain reform through Parliament if possible. What concerned him more was the inequality of wealth and the poverty and inequality of those who made that wealth. He believed that a revolution was inevitable, and although he wanted to minimise violence and avoid a counter-revolution, he 'was on the side of the people' and would have supported them, violent or not.

5

Satire and Drama: 1819–22

The Peterloo Massacre had stimulated Shelley's imagination and he wrote many other political poems during the autumn and winter 1819–20. Mary Shelley said:

> Shelley loved the People; and respected them as often more virtuous, as always more suffering, and therefore more deserving of sympathy, than the great. He believed that a clash between the two classes of society was inevitable, and he eagerly ranged himself on the people's side. He had an idea of publishing a series of poems adapted expressly to commemorate their circumstances and wrongs. (*PW*, p. 588)

Shelley tried to enlist Leigh Hunt's help in publishing this 'series', 'a little volume of *popular songs* wholly political & destined to awaken & direct the imagination of the reformers'.[1] It is not known precisely what poems would have been included, but Mary Shelley mentions 'A New National Anthem' as being one of them. The 'Ballad of the Starving Mother', 'Lines Written during the Castlereagh Administration', 'Song to the Men of England' and 'England in 1819' seem probable. These last three are available in anthologies, the last two being perhaps the best-known of Shelley's political poems after *The Mask of Anarchy*. Among others, 'What Men Gain Fairly' rehearses poetically the argument about entitlement to wealth which Shelley put forward in *A Philosophical View*. The savage 'To Sidmouth and Castlereagh' satirises the politicians by comparing them to birds of prey and to sharks waiting under the slave ship: the 'freight / Is the theme of their debate', the word 'debate' recalling the House of Commons where human life is debated daily as if it is only 'freight', thus the attack is on the whole class, not merely the individuals.

Similarly, 'The Ballad of the Starving Mother' is not only a tale of a hypocritical parson but it also indicts the Church of England which professes Christianity, the religion of love and forgiveness, while condemning illegitimate children and their mothers to starvation in accordance with the views of Malthus.[2]

Leigh Hunt had reviewed Wordsworth's *Peter Bell* in *The Examiner*, about a travelling potter who finds salvation after coming across a faithful ass. He demanded whether Wordsworth really believed that 'his fellow-creatures are to be damned?' J.H. Reynolds, a friend of Keats, wrote a short parody of the poem, *Peter Bell, A Lyrical Ballad*. Shelley's lively imagination took off from there, using Wordsworth's own jog-trotting metre. In *Peter Bell the Third*, the Devil buys Peter's soul for half a crown. Peter works as a footman in Hell, 'a city much like London' (l. 147) – both are ruled by the devil and both are 'populous and smoky' (149), 'small justice shown, and still less pity' (152). 'Lawyers – judges – old hobnobbers [. . .] Bailiffs – Chancellors – Bishops – ' (187–9). Parliament, the stock exchange, the army and the public debt 'Which last is a scheme of Paper money' are familiar Shelleyan targets but in Peter Bell these are joined by hypocritical women 'mewing [. . .] / Of their own virtue, and pursuing / Their gentler sisters to that ruin' (182–5) and seducers who 'lean, and flirt, and stare, and simper' (194). The greed of the rich is also attacked – three verses list their various social engagements all involving food – breakfasts, teas, suppers, lunches and snacks – 'one would furnish forth ten dinners' (207). Everyone in Hell/London leads the society life, and everyone is damned – by themselves. 'The rich are damned beyond all cure' (232). The lightness, energy and comedy of the verse carries the satire on London life into an analysis of how Wordsworth's poetry was affected by his political change of heart. Shelley knew that Wordsworth was so far from his youthful revolutionary beliefs that he had campaigned against the reformer, Henry Brougham, writing pamphlets saying that riches were the only guarantee of political integrity and that the Commons should be chosen by the Lords.[3] Peter Bell's poetry is successful enough for him to give the Devil notice, but the Devil arranges bad reviews. So Peter writes 'enormous folly' (614) for which he is praised and 'odes to the Devil' (635) for which he gets a government position. When the Devil dies, Peter is promoted to his place.

> And yet, a strange and horrid curse
> Clung upon Peter, night and day –
> Month after month the thing grew worse
> And deadlier than in this my verse
> I can find strength to say.
>
> Peter was dull – he was at first
> Dull – O, so dull – so very dull!
> Whether he talked – wrote – or rehearsed -
> Still with this dullness was he cursed –
> Dull – beyond all conception – dull. –
> (698–707)

Peter's writing is so dull that it would 'have made Guatimozin doze / On his red gridiron' (721). Shelley no doubt thought of Guatimozin, an Aztec leader who was tortured on a gridiron by Cortes, because of Cobbett's vow to be tortured on a gridiron if he was wrong. He mentions Cobbett with Castles (really Castle), the spy, and Canning and Castlereagh, the Tory politicians. Cobbett is in the same relation to Castlereagh as Castles is to Canning, which suggests that Cobbett too is a spy. Byron's friend, Hobhouse, suspected this and so did William Hone, who Shelley had admired and to whose defence he had contributed. Shelley enjoyed Cobbett's writing, but he did not trust him and may also have believed him a spy.[4]

Peter Bell the Third connects Shelley's political views expressed in *The Mask of Anarchy* with his feelings about the injustice of the treatment of artists by reviewers who were adherents of the ruling class, showing how political corruption spread through every aspect of life. Although Wordsworth believed himself independent as a poet – he refused to write verses on royal occasions when made Poet Laureate – Shelley seriously accounts for Wordsworth's apostasy since his sinecure was obtained by Lord Lowther, the candidate Wordsworth supported against Brougham. Shelley includes Southey and Coleridge since 'the whole gang', Peacock said, were supporting the Lowthers.

Pisa

Having lost two babies so quickly, the Shelleys wanted to make sure that everything would go well with the new birth. They went to Florence so that Mary could be under the care of a well-known English doctor. Everything went smoothly and Percy Florence, the child who survived them, 'small, but healthy and pretty' was born on 12 November 1819. Shelley said that 'poor Mary begins (for the first time) to look a little consoled' but no one at that time could have understood the seriousness of her depression. Shelley too had suffered. When the Naples baby, Elena, died in June 1820, he felt as if 'the destruction that is consuming me were as an atmosphere which rapt & infected everything connected with me'.[5] Godwin now wanted further financial help, and Shelley had invested money in a project to build a steamboat which Henry Reveley, Maria Gisborne's son, had designed to ply between Livorno and Marseilles. Steamboats had been regularly used on the Clyde and the Thames from 1811, but their development was still in its infancy.[6] Reveley's steamboat was never to be completed, but Shelley took great interest in its possibilities, as he did with scientific and technological innovations. In late January 1820, the Shelleys left Florence for Pisa where they were to settle for the rest of Shelley's life, apart from summers spent at a resort in the Italian style.

During the Napoleonic wars, the Spanish colonies had become economically independent of Spain and shortly after the war, between 1816 and 1821, Venezuela, Colombia, Chile and Argentina declared their political independence. When Ferdinand was restored at the Congress of Vienna, he not only re-established the Spanish Inquisition and a conservative rule in Spain, but wanted to re-conquer his American colonies. But in 1820 army officers on the point of being sent to South America mutinied and instead demanded a constitution. In Naples, where the Carbonari had been active, army officers united with the Carbonari members in a revolution demanding a constitution which the king ('the old pastry

Cook' as Mary Shelley described him) was obliged to grant after his palace soldiers refused to fire on the people.[7] This was followed by a popular uprising in Palermo. Shelley's comments reveal his attitude towards revolutions and towards working people. The news from Palermo was bad in that there was a 'terrible slaughter amounting it is said to 4000 men' but he praised 'the [prodigious] enthusiasm of the inhabitants' especially the women who 'fought from the houses raining down boiling oil on the assailants' and the result 'as it should be – Sicily like Naples is free'.[8] On 26 July, the Kingdom of the Two Sicilies approved a decree suppressing press censorship and elections took place for a Parliament which opened in October. Shelley said that 'the constitutional party' had told the Austrian representative that they were holding the royal family hostage lest Austria should intervene, a 'necessary, & most just measure when the forces of the combatants as well as the merits of their respective causes are so unequal! That kings should be every where hostages for liberty were admirable!'[9] Even so, Shelley did not believe that the Austrians would succeed if the Neapolitans stood firm. Writing to Claire, who had reported a disparaging remark of Sgricci's, he said:

> They cannot improvise tragedies as Sgricci can, but is it certain that under no excitement they would be incapable of more enthusiasm for their country? Besides it is not of them we speak, but of the people of the Kingdom of Naples, the cultivators of the soil; whom a sudden & great impulse might awaken into citizens and men, as the French & Spaniards have been awakened & may render instruments of a system of future social life before which the existing anarchies of Europe will be dissolved & absorbed. [. . .] – As to the Austrians I doubt not they are strong men, well disciplined, obeying the master motion like the wheels of a perfect engine: they may even have, as men, more individual excellence & perfection (not that I believe it) than the Neapolitans, – but all these things if the spirit of Regeneration is abroad are chaff before the storm, the very elements & events will fight against them.[10]

He believed, therefore, in the power of a revolution to change those involved and the possibility of a determined people winning against a colonial oppressor, something which was seen later, for example, in the twentieth-century struggle of the Vietnamese against the United States. He also shows his respect for and his faith in the abilities of the Neapolitans, speaking of them in much the same terms as he spoke of the English agricultural workers and identifying himself far more than he had done before with Italians. As for royalty, Shelley indicated his utter contempt for them. Although a revolution took place in Piedmont in March 1821, Shelley did not celebrate it with poetry or follow it in his correspondence as he did the Neapolitan, which suggests a closer personal involvement with Naples. His *Ode to Naples* recalls the beauty of Pompeii and the ocean, and hopes that Naples will be imitated by other Italian states and that the Neapolitan revolutionaries would stand firm against the Austrians:

> Nor let thy high heart fail,
> Though from their hundred gates the leagued Oppressors
> With hurried legions move!
> (73-75, *PW*, p. 618)

Byron had fallen in love with an Italian countess, Teresa Guiccioli, who had left her husband for him. Teresa had obtained a legal separation on the condition she lived with her father, Count Ruggero Gamba and brother, Pietro. They were both Carbonari members and Byron himself became involved. They believed that Naples would be followed by a general Italian uprising. But the Austrians invaded Italy in 1821, defeated the Neapolitan constitutionalists and restored the king to his former powers on March 24. Revolts in other parts of Italy were forestalled. The Gambas were exiled and on 21 April, the Austrians defeated the Piedmontese revolution too. Teresa said, 'Now the Italians must go back to making opera'.[11]

Swellfoot the Tyrant

English politics became intertwined with the Neapolitan revolution in an incident which sparked off Shelley's next political drama. The reform movement in England was at a standstill. In this mood, radicals supported an unusual cause – that of George IV's Queen

Caroline, whom George was attempting to divorce and prevent being crowned queen. The Shelleys were staying for the summer at San Giuliano Terme, a resort near Pisa. Claire was staying at Livorno and with friends came on a day trip to see them. Shelley began to read his guests what is thought to have been his *Ode to Naples*. It was market day and there were pigs for sale below in the market place so Shelley's reading was accompanied by grunts. He thought of the great comedy by Aristophanes with its chorus of frogs, and was inspired to write a Greek comedy in the style of Aristophanes, *Swellfoot the Tyrant*, about the royal scandal.[12]

Earlier, Shelley had not shown much interest in the Queen Caroline affair, writing to the Gisbornes 'It is really time for the English to wean themselves from this nonsense, for really their situation is too momentous to justify them in attending to Punch and his Wife'.[13] Yet in England, Caroline's cause was immensely popular especially with women. The king's serial adulteries were well known; he had even been secretly married at the time of his marriage to Caroline and he had had a succession of mistresses. He had earlier attempted a 'delicate investigation' into Caroline's morals claiming she had had an illegitimate child but this came to nothing when the child's real mother was produced. The government had nonetheless tried to prevent the publication of this report. George and Caroline were now separated and she had been travelling in Italy. Spies were sent there to gather evidence of her adultery. It was collected in a green bag, as was the case with treasonable offences and the case was to be tried in Parliament. Caroline returned to England to defend herself. Radicals, even Carlile, were supporting her, believing that they could unite around this cause in the absence of reform activity and in the repressive situation in which they now found themselves. Cobbett was writing the queen's material and she became the house guest of Matthew Wood, MP for the City of London and a reformer. Hone now collaborated with Cruikshank again in *The Queen's Matrimonial Ladder*. There were so many brilliant caricatures of the affair that the king spent £2,600 to buy off the caricaturists and arranged for anti-Caroline cartoons to be issued.[14]

Shelley's style and imagery in *Swellfoot the Tyrant* shows his familiarity with the radical press cartoons. 'Swellfoot' is a literal

Figure 7 The Radical Ladder by George Cruikshank. (Photograph by William Alderson, kind permission of John Gardner)

translation of 'Oedipus', the king in the tragedy, *Oedipus Tyrannus*, by Sophocles but also refers to George IV's gout.[15] The chorus in *Swellfoot* are pigs, the 'swinish multitude', and the spies are a supernatural Gadfly, Leech (the Chairman of the spying Milan Commission was a Sir John Leach) and Rat. Parliament is represented as a Council of Wizards led by Mammon (Prime Minister, Lord Liverpool), who produces paper money by magic. 'Council of Wizards' is appropriate as the defenders of the unreformed Parliament claimed that the MPs for rotten boroughs 'virtually' represented people while Shelley believed that they 'actually represent a deception and a shadow, virtually represent none but the powerful and the rich'.[16] The other wizards include Purganax, a literal translation of Castlereagh's name, Laoctonos, suggesting the Spartan (the Duke of Wellington, combining his warrior status and his plain, direct style) and Dakry, or Tear (Lord Eldon, the Lord Chancellor who wept when he pronounced the death sentence and who had decided the future of Shelley and Harriet's children). Swellfoot is the obese, greedy, licentious George IV, and Iona is Queen Caroline.

The play is a comedy in the style of Aristophanes, the Greek dramatist who wrote at the time of the Athenians' war with Sparta. Like Aristophanes, Shelley writes beautiful poetic passages as well as zany, bawdy satirical humour and the situation is both tragic, because it reflects the situation of English people, and comic because they are depicted as pigs. Illustrating the link between hypocritical religion and tyranny, the opening scene parodies the first scene of *Oedipus* with king, temple and supplicating, starving subjects, but Swellfoot is admiring his 'kingly paunch', worshipping his goddess, Famine, and ignoring the supplicating pigs. Then, refusing their pleas, he calls for Solomon, the royal porkman and Zephaniah, the hog-butcher, the free market economists (Adam Smith and David Ricardo) and Moses the sow-gelder (Malthus). Ricardo was of Jewish origin but Shelley makes them all Jews in a racist slur emphasising their hypocrisy in being willing to slaughter non-kosher meat. It is discreditable that Shelley is less generous than the more conservative playwright Richard Cumberland, whose play *The Jew* was performed at Drury Lane in 1794 in order to counter the stereotype of the grasping Jewish moneylender. Swellfoot, however, gives the bloodthirsty orders.

When Zephaniah says that that the boar which Swellfoot orders to be killed because he is overfed, is suffering from dropsy, Swellfoot replies, ''Tis all the same' (I, 86) and tries to sell the rest to Solomon who begins to protest. Swellfoot says:

> Kill them out of the way
> That shall be price enough, and let me hear
> Their everlasting grunts and whines no more!
> (I, 93–5)

Shelley believed that Jews behaved as they did because they had no choice in their oppressed circumstances and elsewhere considered 're-establishing the antient free republic' of the Jews.[17]

Shelley satirises the economic situation and the ruthless prosecution of forgers of paper money when Mammon marries his daughter, Banknotina, to the gallows and produces 'little gibbets' (I, 213) but the centre of the play is the struggle between the pigs and the rulers. Mammon fears Iona's return because he thinks that the pigs will realise that they are descended from the 'free' Minotaur, a half-bull, half-man of Greek legend; they 'still / call themselves Bulls, though thus degenerate' (I, 140–141) and Iona may inspire them to claim their own freedom. Iona must have a show trial, and, referring to the creation of peerages in order to pass the Act of Union in 1801,[18] Purganax suggests:

> . . . fattening some few in two separate sties,
> And giving them clean straw, tying some bits
> Of ribbon round their legs – giving their Sows
> Some tawdry lace . . . .
> (I, 296–9)

The Wizards' 'GREEN BAG' is full of poison which will turn innocence to guilt, just like the spy system, and the contents will be poured on Iona. Purganax will handle it as 'I have been used to / Handle all sorts of poisons' (I, 380–1). Shelley's ironic comment on English 'morality' is that being the 'Lover of other wives and husbands than their own' is 'the heaviest sin on this side of the Alps!' (I, 370–1).

Laoctonos reports that the pigs have rescued Iona and bribed the 'ape-guards' who refused to fire on them. The soldiers were sympathetic to Caroline and this reflects Shelley's hope that they and the people would unite. Truth is manipulated by the spin doctor, Purganax, who makes beautiful speeches to the assembled Boars in the Public Sty (House of Commons) about the Queen's innocence while hinting at her guilt. But it's to no avail as the doors are 'staved in' and 'a number of exceedingly lean PIGS and SOWS and BOARS rush in' (stage direction, p. 403).

Iona's trial is set for the Feast of Famine, at a magnificent banquet (for Swellfoot and his party, hog-wash for the rest) in Famine's temple. But before they come in, the goddess, Liberty, enters and prays to Famine to become her ally, to 'wake the multitude' but to 'lead them not upon the paths of blood' (II, 90–1). Just before Iona undergoes her test she snatches the 'GREEN BAG' from Purganax and pours it over 'Swellfoot and his whole Court' (stage direction, p. 408). They are transformed into foxes, badgers, hares, wolves and otters, which in Shelley's day would have been considered vermin – an excellent image for the government. 'The image of FAMINE then arises with a tremendous sound' and 'the PIGS begin scrambling for the loaves' (stage direction, p. 408) behind the altar. A MINOTAUR appears. He is really John Bull (a term for the English people) and if Iona mounts him 'at least till you have hunted down your game' (II,114), he will not throw her. It seems that the Minotaur will get rid of Iona when she has got rid of the court, as Shelley hoped that the unity around Caroline would lead to a revolution which would get rid of all royalty.

Iona climbs on the Minotaur's back and rides off with some of the pigs in pursuit of the former court, singing a hunting song. Significantly, the pigs who have eaten the loaves are turned into 'BULLS' and they sit quietly behind the altar. These are perhaps the few who 'aspire to more' of Shelley's *Philosophical View* who will lead the movement towards a republic and equality and in fact it is a comic and poetic version of Shelley's main message: the corruption and greed of the ruling class is starving the people; they should unite, win over the soldiers, and act at once.

This time he didn't bother to send it to Ollier or Leigh Hunt but asked Horace Smith to publish it anonymously for him. Smith did so, but when only seven copies had been sold 'a burly alderman called upon me' to demand the name of the author, in order that he might be prosecuted for a seditious and disloyal libel' by the Society for the Suppression of Vice. For the sake of the printer, James Johnston, Smith 'submitted to this insolent dictation' and allowed the copies to be destroyed.[19] It is a shame that more people did not see this play, which has been on the whole neglected ever since and probably never performed, although it would be very successful on stage.[20]

Hellas

At Pisa, the Shelleys' way of life became more social and began to take on more of an Italian flavour. They went riding, visited the opera and went to the masked ball which concluded the Carnival. Although at first their only friends in Pisa were Lady Mountcashell and her lover George Tighe, they made others, among them some Italians: Professor Pacchiani, Teresa Viviani and Tommaso Sgricci, an *improvvisatore*. *Improvvisatori*, as their name suggests, gave performances of improvised poetry and Shelley wrote a review of Sgricci's performance. Sgricci was exceptionally talented and admired. He had a political commitment to Italy's liberation, saying in one performance: 'I see the Alps grow – and the sea rise and become agitated in order to impede the enemies.'[21]

Shelley wanted the freedom to pay attention to other women like Sophia Stacey, a family connection who visited them in Florence or Teresa Viviani. Mary Shelley referred mockingly to his relationship with Teresa as his 'Italian platonics'. Mary was entitled to the same freedom and she had a parallel flirtation with the future Prime Minister of Greece, Alexandros Mavrokordatos, whom she described as 'an amiable, young, agreeable and learned Greek prince'. He came every morning to give her Greek lessons and she in turn taught him English. As he was 'exceedingly clever' he learnt it 'in only four months'.[22]

Mavrokordatos belonged to a wealthy and influential Greek family. Well-educated Greeks had opportunities for advancement under the Ottoman Empire; they had positions in government service, as merchants and in shipping, and the Orthodox Church had privileges.

There were large Greek communities in Western European cities, among them Livorno. The idea of an independent Greece emerged from these communities under the influence of Western European ideals of ancient Greece, ideals which meant nothing to the modern Greeks who were unaware of that history. Mavrokordatos had been a student at the University of Pisa and subsequently acted as secretary to the government of Wallachia, a Turkish province on the Danube, now part of Romania. His uncle was the governor. In 1819 problems arose between his uncle and the Ottoman Empire and the two of them fled first to Geneva and then to Pisa. Mavrokordatos believed that a war between Turkey and Russia was inevitable and that Turkey would lose. He felt that an independent Greece would have a future role in holding the balance of power in Europe. Greeks in Russia had started a movement for revolution in Greece. When a local Ottoman ruler, Ali Pasha, rebelled against Constantinople, the expatriate groups seized the opportunity and began collecting arms, building up a treasury and making gunpowder. In April 1821 news arrived that Alexandros Ypsilantis had crossed into Wallachia with a small troop to join other local military commanders. The Shelleys, with the help of Mavrokordatos and presumably at his request, wrote letters to *The Examiner* and to the *Morning Chronicle* enclosing a proclamation 'declaring the liberty of Greece'. It added 'The Turks are completely driven from the Morea'.[23]

This was not true. Ypsilantis' rebellion failed and the struggle in the Peloponnese ('the Morea') would go on for some time; a tragic and savage civil war with terrible atrocities on both sides. Greeks massacred Turks, Turks massacred Greeks, yet these communities had been living alongside each other harmoniously for centuries. Many Turks spoke only Greek and Turkish garrisons in the peninsula had fallen into disuse as there had been no need for them. Although the Greeks had genuine grievances against the government, it was their neighbours who suffered. As a result of Ypsilantis' action, Greek quarters in cities such as Smyrna (Izmir) were attacked, the Orthodox Patriarch, Mavrokordatos' uncle, was hanged and bishops and archbishops and many ordinary Greeks who had not rebelled were executed. In May 1821, Mavrokordatos sailed for Greece with a group of Italian volunteers. Because the revolutions in Naples and

Piedmont had been put down, many of the Carbonari wanted to fight in Greece either because they had no choice, being wanted men, or because they felt that continuing the struggle in Greece successfully might give them a chance of reigniting it in Italy.[24]

In February 1821, Shelley had jotted down some ideas and sketches for a drama about Greek independence, but had not continued with it. In order to raise awareness of Greece in England, he took these up and wrote the drama *Hellas*. He asked Ollier to publish it straightaway, dedicated it to Mavrokordatos and quoted from Sophocles's *Oedipus at Colonus*, 'This day shall victory bring' (p. 805). Although Shelley did not personally care for Mavrokordatos, he admired his talent and character and thought that he would 'probably fill a high rank in the magistracy of the infant republic'. Mavrokordatos had taken the Shelleys into his confidence and when he discussed politics with them he was influenced by Shelley's ideas. While Greece would not even be a republic, let alone as enlightened as Shelley hoped, Mavrokordatos became far more liberal in his views than could have been expected from his earlier career and this has been attributed to the influence of Shelley.[25]

Shelley based *Hellas* on Aeschylus' drama *The Persians*. In doing so, he was making a political point. He believed that 'human endeavour' had reached its highest point so far in the democratic republic of fifth century Athens, both politically and in artistic achievement, and an example of this was its drama: ' . . . the art itself never was understood or practiced according to the philosophy of it, as at Athens' (p. 683). The Athenians themselves thought *The Persians* a significant political play; Aristophanes' *The Frogs* describes it as 'an effective sermon on the will to win'.[26]

Shelley structured *Hellas* in the same way as *The Persians*. Both are set in the court of the tyrant, *Hellas* in the Sultan's harem in Constantinople and Aeschylus' play in the Persian court at Susa. In *The Persians*, Queen Atossa, the mother of King Xerxes, is awaiting news of her son and his grand army. She has a bad dream, sees a bad omen, and through a religious sacrifice raises the spirit of her dead husband to forecast the future. A herald brings the news that the huge army has been defeated by the much smaller Greek force and then Xerxes returns to lament his disgrace at being beaten by a people

who are 'slaves to none'.[27] In *Hellas*, Sultan Mahmud also has a bad
dream and wants to see the Wandering Jew, Ahasuerus. He believes
Ahasuerus can tell him the future. Ahasuerus tells him political
power is ephemeral. Mahmud imagines he sees the spirit of his
ancestor, Mahomet II, who had won Constantinople and Mahomet
convinces him that empires fall as well as rise. Shelley makes it
clear that there is nothing supernatural about Mahmud's vision, or
Ahasuerus' prophecy; these are psychological effects. Ahasuerus
is 'tempting Mahmud to that state of mind in which ideas may be
supposed to assume the force of sensations' (p. 586). Nevertheless
there is a sense throughout the drama of forces beyond the control of
any of its characters. Messengers bring news of Greek victories, and
speak of the Greeks' defiant spirit even in defeat, expressing 'the will
to win' also shown by Shelley's chorus of Greek slave girls who sing
of Greece's past greatness in choruses which depict their Christian
faith. Shelley's hatred of the system which produces this struggle is
clear from the lines:

> The world is weary of the past,
> O might it die or rest at last!
> (1100–01)

At the end of the drama, the result of the struggle is inconclusive;
Shelley did not know whether the Greeks would win, and in fact
much of the 'newspaper erudition' he had was inaccurate. But
whether or not the Greeks won this struggle, Shelley believed that
the Greek ideas would persist. He said that 'circumstances make men
what they are [. . .] our character is determined by events'. Byron had
known a Greek who seemed 'a timid and unenterprising person' who
now commanded 'the insurgents in Attica' (p. 585).

Unlike his battle over *Laon and Cythna*, he told Ollier, 'If any
passages should alarm you in the notes, you are at liberty to suppress
them'.[28] Ollier did suppress a paragraph in the Preface, beginning
'Should the English people ever become free' in which Shelley
suggests that the struggle in Greece will inspire the English to fight.
'This is the age of the war of the oppressed against the oppressors',
Shelley continued. He believed that the revolutions in Spain and

Figure 8   Illustration to *Hellas* Scene 1 from *The Poetical Works of Percy Bysshe Shelley* (London: Milne and Sowerby). (Photograph by William Alderson, kind permission of Nora Crook)

Italy and Greece would inspire the rest of Europe to put down 'every one of those ringleaders of the privileged gangs of murderers and swindlers, called Sovereigns' (p. 550). To a certain extent he was right: in 1830 there would be revolutions in France, Belgium, Poland and the Netherlands followed by the 1848 'year of revolution'. Greece would be declared independent by 1832 and in 1861 Italy would become a united independent nation. Shelley, however, would have thought of this as only a step towards freedom since they were not the democratic republics that he envisaged. After all, England was a nation state and he did not believe the English people to be free.

New Friends

Shelley had asked friends like Smith, Peacock, Hunt and Hogg to come and visit him and was pleased when Tom Medwin, his second cousin from Horsham who had been in the army in India, joined them. Medwin had friends who were interested in meeting Shelley, Jane and Edward Williams and Edward Trelawny. The Williamses arrived to live in Pisa in January, and they became friends although neither Shelley nor Mary thought Jane 'very clever' at first.[29] She had left a violent husband in India for Edward; they were not married but they had a son, Edward, and a daughter, Rosalind, named after Shelley's poem, *Rosalind and Helen*. Despite first impressions, Shelley became very attracted to Jane and wrote her a number of beautiful lyrics.

He had got a little boat in order to explore the canals around Pisa. Edward Williams, who managed to capsize it on one occasion, was often his companion, and he celebrated one trip with an unfinished poem, *The Boat on the Serchio*. On another occasion, he sailed down the river and went by sea to Livorno.[30] Claire was away and the Williamses and the Shelleys spent the summer at San Giuliano Terme. With them, Shelley apparently best achieved his desire of living in a group relationship.

Shelley and Byron

Despite his interest in Greece and Italy, Shelley's mind turned to a potential solution for the problems of getting published in England,

Figure 9 From *Eton Sketched* by Quis? Epoch III. The Remove 1. Poet's Walk. (Photograph by William Alderson, kind permission of Angus Graham-Campbell)

Figure 10 From *Eton Sketched* by Quis? Epoch III. The Remove 2. Towing up to Surley. (Photograph by William Alderson, kind permission of Angus Graham-Campbell)

a problem which Byron shared in the case of *Don Juan*. Shelley was also concerned about Allegra. Byron wished her to be brought up a Catholic, educated in a convent and married to a suitable Italian nobleman. Although the Shelleys and Claire would not have agreed with this scheme, there was nothing they could do since Claire had given up the little girl to her father. Shelley hoped to persuade him to allow Claire to see Allegra; in any case, Byron wanted to see Shelley, who went to Ravenna to visit him in August, stopping in Livorno en route to spend his birthday sailing in the harbour with Claire.

Teresa and her family were in Florence and were thinking of going to Switzerland but Byron was afraid that if he joined them in either place they would be targeted by gossiping English communities. Shelley suggested they all came to Pisa instead, and agreed to find Byron a suitable house and to write to Teresa and persuade her of the plan. Byron agreed to Shelley's idea of inviting the experienced editor Leigh Hunt to come to Italy and edit a journal to be called *The Liberal*, in which they could publish their work without fear of censorship and give a voice in opposition to right-wing journals like the *Quarterly Review*. Byron's name would attract a readership.

Byron took time to move his large household, including a number of pet animals. Teresa and her family were already in Pisa when he arrived in November. Leigh Hunt was supposed to be on his way. Unfortunately, his wife became ill before they left England and they wintered in Plymouth and did not arrive until the following June. Horace Smith was also en route to Italy but, sadly, in France his wife too fell ill and they remained there. Claire returned to Florence to avoid Byron.

When Byron arrived, Shelley was obliged to lead a more social life. Byron had weekly dinners at which Shelley complained his nerves were 'shaken to pieces by sitting up, contemplating the rest making themselves vats of claret &c. till 3 o'Clock in the morning'. But Shelley also found Byron's constant companionship of 'the understanding & the imagination' 'no small relief'.[31] Byron supported Shelley in a plan to rescue an atheist whom they heard was to be burnt in neighbouring Lucca. It turned out to be unnecessary.[32] Shelley and Williams made use of Byron's billiard table, and most afternoons they rode with a group out of town to practise pistol shooting. Shelley and Byron were better shots than the others, Shelley slightly better than Byron.[33] The authorities would not allow this practice in town; after all, the group included Carbonari. It has been suggested that Shelley was unaware of and uninvolved in local politics when the city was in a state of 'ferment and unrest' and many students and professors at the university were major activists in the struggle for freedom.[34] It would be strange if Shelley, knowing Mavrokordatos and Pacchiani, knew nothing of the political situation but he may have been cautious in correspondence.

According to Williams, Byron thought Shelley by far the most imaginative poet of the day and sought his advice. Shelley was beginning to feel inferior to Byron, thinking that Byron's poetry had had the success and fame his talent deserved whereas his own poetry was not well reviewed or widely read. Yet, in January 1822, Shelley began writing what would have been a masterpiece; a play, *Charles the First*.[35]

Charles the First

Charles I ruled for eleven years without a Parliament and raised money by unfair taxes, culminating in the infamous Ship money tax which, originally intended to be levied on coastal towns to defend them from piracy, was extended to inland areas such as Buckinghamshire, where John Hampden refused to pay it. Queen Henrietta Maria, was ostentatious in her Catholic devotion and her chapel was theatrical in splendour. William Laud, Archbishop of Canterbury, was determined to root out Puritanism in the Anglican Church and sentenced Puritans to imprisonment and mutilations such as ears and nose being cut off. Laud returned the communion table, which had been placed centrally, to its position facing east as in the Catholic Church and re-installed altar rails. Charles's attempt to impose an Anglican prayer book on the Scottish Kirk led to war with Scotland. These events and a scene in which Cromwell and other opponents of the king are prevented from emigrating to America, are covered by the four scenes which Shelley completed for the play. The reactionary and repressive nature of Charles's reign was echoed in Shelley's Europe.

Since 1818, Shelley had been reading English Civil War memoirs and histories by David Hume, whom he described as a 'Tory', and Catherine Macaulay, known to be of liberal views and admired by Mary Wollstonecraft. Given his view of monarchy, especially of Charles, in *A Philosophical View*, the play would have been designed to counter the Oak Apple Day propaganda and rehabilitate the 'calumniated Republicans'.[36] Shelley's characters included Hampden, John Pym, Oliver Cromwell and Sir Henry Vane the Younger. He believed that the play was 'not coloured by the party spirit of the author'[37] as he would portray Charles not just as a political tyrant but also as a loving husband, father and connoisseur of the arts, a view supported by one of his sources, Lucy Hutchinson. She described Charles as 'temperate chaste and serious' but 'a worse encroacher upon the civil and spiritual liberties of his people by far than his father'.[38] This was a more sophisticated approach to tyranny than the plain evil of *The Cenci*. Charles had a jester, Archibald Armstrong, and, like the Fool in *King Lear*, Shelley's court jester, Archy, comments ironically on the foolishness of Charles's actions.

Although Shelley shows the courage and defiance of the Puritans, he was not sympathetic to the puritanical forbidding of art and amusement and regarded Cromwell as a betrayer of the English Revolution, as Bonaparte was of the French. The Putney debates were not available to him. He would not have known of the Diggers either, but he would have learnt of John Lilburne and the Levellers from his sources. The term 'leveller', either as abuse or as a badge of pride, was used in Shelley's day and would have been likely to attract his attention. Perhaps Shelley would have emphasised the political importance of the crowd by giving them a role.

Spectacular scenes were popular in the contemporary theatre and Viganò's ballets usually opened with a large crowd scene. Shelley's play opens with a spectacular scene based on a real event. A procession of young lawyers from the Inns of Court travelled to Whitehall to present a masque for the queen, also intended as a protest with an anti-masque of beggars to indicate the condition of the country. The crowd, waiting for this procession, discuss whether or not the masque is sinful and what they think of the king and the government. A king's servant enters and rudely pushes the people about to make room for the king, something Mary Shelley described happening when the Emperor of Austria visited Rome in 1818.[39] The royal party enters. They simply cross the stage in silence without cheers from the crowd or a word from the king. A Puritan, Leighton, enters. He has been branded and had his nose slit and ears mutilated. This juxtaposition of tyrant and victim, as well as the masque and anti-masque, are a metaphor for the country as a whole. The audience hears what the common people are saying before they hear what the rulers say or even the leading opponents to the regime. This is probably the first scene in English drama where the protagonist is the crowd.

Although Shelley did not finish *Charles*, he probably would have returned to it after his summer break, given the amount of research he had done and the high quality of the dialogue. He may have intended it for Covent Garden, whose manager had refused *The Cenci* but had said he would take any other play from the author. If Shelley had completed and sent it in 1822 it would have been timely since the theatre commissioned Mary Mitford's *Charles the First* in 1825. By that time, there was a new Examiner of Plays who banned it, but it is possible that Shelley's play might have been passed by the former Examiner. Mitford's play was performed ten years later at the Victoria (now the Old Vic).[40]

Williams's friend, Edward Trelawny, arrived and told them colourful, though invented, stories of his life. Trelawny had picturesque looks and had created a past to match, but his life had been much duller. He wrote *Recollections of the Last Days of Byron and Shelley* in 1858 and, 20 years later, *Records of Shelley, Byron and the Author*, which include some unreliable tales. One of these, also told by Jane Williams, is of Shelley taking her and her two small children out in a boat when he decided to 'solve the great mystery', in other words to drown them all, but she, with her common-sense reasoning, said that they all needed their dinner first and managed to get him to row back to shore.[41] Yet Edward Williams does not mention the incident in his journal, although, according to the story, Jane told him about it when she reached the shore, vowing not to go in a boat with Shelley again. It sounds more like a dinner party anecdote than a factual account. Trelawny also describes an attempt to teach Shelley to swim, claiming that he plunged to the bottom of the pool and lay 'stretched out on the bottom like a conger eel, not making the least attempt to save himself'.[42] This is clearly impossible since a body would rise to the surface in such circumstances. Trelawny's friend, Captain Roberts, agreed to build a boat for Byron, the *Bolivar*, and a small one for Shelley and Williams, the *Don Juan*. They planned to spend the summer sailing in the Gulf of Spezia.

Returning from the pistol shooting one evening, one of the party was jostled by a soldier, causing his horse to rear and to collide with Byron's. They chased after the man and Shelley, who was the first to reach him, asked him to explain his action. The man only cursed Shelley. The others caught up and Shelley moved his horse directly between the soldier and the others in an attempt to prevent violence. He was knocked to the ground and, dizzy and sick, took no further part. When the soldier, Masi, rode by Byron's palace, someone on Byron's staff struck him with a lance. Masi was taken to hospital, not expected to live.[43] He recovered, but the authorities responded by exiling the Gambas once more. Byron was to go with them. The strangeness of the provocation suggests that the authorities had planned this.

Meanwhile, Claire had been worried about Allegra and had schemes of kidnapping her. Shelley tried to persuade Byron to transfer the child to a convent at Lucca where they could visited her more easily, but Byron refused. Claire's instinct was right; Allegra died of typhus. To avoid Claire meeting Byron, the Shelleys and the Williamses moved to Lerici on the Gulf of Spezia where they shared a house; it was difficult for them to find accommodation, perhaps because of the Masi incident. When Claire was eventually told about Allegra, she became quite calm, but all these upsets had a terrible effect on both the Shelleys. Shelley began to experience the nightmares, sleepwalking and hallucinations once more and Mary was not 'well in body or mind', which resulted in a nearly fatal miscarriage.[44] Having another baby might have helped Mary to gradually recover her health and spirits, but after this fourth loss she became worse. She began to hate Lerici. She wrote Hunt a letter begging him not to come there, saying she wished she could 'break my chains and leave this dungeon'.[45] On the other hand, although Shelley had thought of suicide and asked Trelawny to procure him some prussic acid to keep by him,[46] his health began to improve through sailing, the beauty of the bay and the comforting presence and musical talent of Jane Williams. He began working on a great poem, *The Triumph of Life*.

Last Journeys

Shelley sailed to meet the Hunts in Livorno on 1 July, with Williams and a young boatman, Charles Vivian. Shelley rushed into Hunt's arms, exclaiming that he was 'so inexpressibly delighted!' to see him.[47] He took Hunt sightseeing, and arranged manuscripts for *The Liberal*. Byron was still enthusiastic about the journal, and Shelley's trip, although difficult and harassing, was a success. On 8 July he and Williams set off for Lerici with a boatload of stores, money and wine for the Lerici harbourmaster. The weather was fine and the wind right. Three hours later, off Viareggio, a storm blew up. The *Don Juan* sank and the three men were drowned. Yachtsmen with 25 years' experience of Mediterranean sailing, who know the Viareggio region well, say that very sudden storms occur there which are impossible to forecast and which would have overwhelmed a boat such as the *Don Juan*. Local sturdy feluccas, whose sailors were used to the weather conditions, were more likely to survive.

Trelawny presented a portrait of Shelley as an incompetent sailor, telling a story of Williams teaching Shelley how to steer.[48] Yet Shelley would not have needed lessons. If he had not sailed earlier on Warnham Pond, near Horsham, he had been around boats at least since he was ten at Syon House. Although a freshwater sailor, he had also in the past couple of years sailed down to Livorno, in Livorno harbour and in the bay of Lerici. It is difficult to believe that anyone who loved sailing as much as Shelley did – he doodled boats all over his manuscripts and even dreamed about it – would not know how to steer.[49] Trelawny's stories gained currency because of the accident. On the other hand, Roberts had altered the boat to make her carry more sail and, while this was not a problem when they were sailing in the bay, it could have been disastrous when they sailed back from Livorno. Furthermore, Roberts and Trelawny frequently altered their accounts of what happened to the *Don Juan*.[50]

The bodies were washed up near Viareggio on July 18 and, as they had to be cremated for quarantine reasons, Trelawny devised a ceremony on the seashore on 16 August. Hunt and Byron were present, but women did not attend funerals in those days, so Mary was not. Shelley's ashes were buried in Rome in the non-Catholic cemetery on 15 January 1823. He had not lived to be 30.

6

The Legacy of a Revolutionary

A book about Shelley's political life and writing cannot possibly do justice to the full range of his interests which was vast: science and technology, including botany and biology and medicine, philosophy, psychology and metaphysics, art, drama and literature. His poetry and such essays as *On Life* reflect these interests. His political thinking was, therefore, not narrow or limited to one aspect such as reform of parliament, but a way of thinking about how people should live their lives and the need for a just and equal society. His conclusion was that it would require a revolution to bring it about. The problem lay in how this revolution should be achieved.

A Philosophical View of Reform suggests that although a democratic republic should be established gradually to avoid bloodshed, the ruling class would probably never allow the first steps to be taken, let alone give up their position and wealth. This would make revolution inevitable. Shelley realised that a revolution had to be a movement of the whole people and he thought that the flaw of the French Revolution was its violence, since it became endemic in society, prevented the new society coming into being and led to Bonaparte's 1799 *coup d'état*. This achieved the very antithesis of what the Revolution stood for by replacing one tyranny with another. But, although aspects of Shelley's thought could be used to support pacifist views, he did not reject violence in all circumstances. In this, he differed from the Quakers to whom he owed much in his own political education. He was on the side of the revolutionaries even if violence ensued, realising that the ruling class perpetrated violence on a massive scale both on a day-to-day basis and in a counter-revolution. He showed this in his support for revolutions when they did happen, even if, as in Greece, they used violent means. It is unlikely that Shelley knew quite how tragic the results of these were, but he did know that there were massacres.[1]

Shelley was inspired in his early years by the Foxite Whigs and the Quakers, the American Declaration of Independence and the 1793 constitution which Babeuf described as 'the true law of the French'.[2] He drew from many political writers: Rousseau, Wollstonecraft, Godwin, Paine, Spence and, probably, Babeuf, perhaps through Italian sources.[3] Owen, Leigh Hunt and Cobbett also influenced his ideas. He was on the side of Luddites, O'Connellites, the reform movement and the Carbonari in Italy. He supported revolutions as they took place from Mexico to Naples and Greece.

In Naples, Piedmont and Spain the revolutionaries had demanded a constitution. Shelley supported their demands as a first step. He thought that as people won more they would demand more until the kind of republic described in *A Philosophical View* was achieved. He supported reform of Parliament in England and Catholic Emancipation in Ireland as steps towards this republic not ends in themselves, but he deplored the time that the reformers wasted fighting each other when they needed to be united and clear on what they were demanding. He thought it better to demand something achievable before swiftly pressing for more so in the first instance he rejected demands which he personally agreed with such as universal suffrage. He realised that delay meant that the ruling class had an opportunity to co-ordinate their attacks as they did in 1819. He did not want an 'immature attempt at a republic', because the ruling class would have the power over the military machine and would be able to crush it. Like Trotsky, Shelley wanted it 'rendered permanent' (p. 664). At a time when working people were just beginning to see themselves as a class, Shelley saw that there were two classes, working people and a 'double aristocracy' of the rich which exploited them. He was not alone in understanding that wealth was created by workers' labour. Henry Hunt thought that they deserved a share of it. But Shelley knew they deserved all of it, shared equally and emphasised that they could and should unite to get what they created. He did not expect to achieve these aims with a reform of Parliament, but he did not expect political activity to stand still or go backwards after these aims had been achieved.

Shelley died too early to be even a Utopian socialist, as Owen's and Fournier's experiments were still in the future, and certainly too early to be a Marxist. Yet the left has often claimed him because of his insights into class struggle. Shelley championed the freedom of the press as part of the political education of the workers, writing letters in support of Eaton and Carlile and contributing towards Hone's defence in 1817. It is fitting that, although it is often said that Shelley had no influence in his lifetime, Carlile published the *Declaration of Rights* and Carlile's employee, William Clark, published a pirated edition of *Queen Mab* in 1821. *Queen Mab* went through at least a dozen such editions during the next decade and Shelley's work reached a working class readership. The radical press was to have an impact on Shelley's reputation as a poet in academic circles.

Sir Timothy Shelley had forced Mary Shelley to withdraw her 1824 edition of Shelley's poems by threatening to cut off her allowance but, since there were so many pirated editions, he was obliged to permit her to publish Shelley's collected works 15 years later. A new generation of poets, including Robert Browning and Alfred Tennyson, admired him, to be followed by Edgar Allan Poe, Algernon Charles Swinburne and Thomas Hardy. By the end of the century, Shelley was established as a major British poet. Public appetite for a biography increased as his reputation grew. Mary Shelley's *Notes* to the poems circumvented Sir Timothy's veto on writing a memoir by including some biographical details, but they glossed over his controversial marital life. The memoirs of friends such as Hunt, Medwin, Trelawny, Hogg, and Peacock were less discreet. They sometimes showed him as almost a saint, sometimes as rather ridiculous, exaggerating characteristics of absent-mindedness and impulsiveness.

Queen Mab became known as 'the Chartists' Bible' and, as Engels remembered to Eleanor Marx, 'We all knew Shelley by heart then'.[4] Marx himself admired Shelley, saying that, 'he was essentially a revolutionist and he would always have been one of the advanced guard of socialism'.[5] Anna Wheeler, the companion of William Thompson both of whom came to share many of Shelley's ideas, quoted, slightly inaccurately, 'Shall man be free and woman a slave'.[6] By the latter part of the nineteenth century, Shelley's Cythna had become a guiding star of the women's movement. Dr Richard Pankhurst, husband of

Emmeline and father of Christabel, Sylvia and Adela, and grandfather of William Thompson's biographer, 'talked of Shelley' to his children and Sylvia, the artist, decorated a hall dedicated to her father with quotations from *The Revolt of Islam*.[7] The suffragettes' slogan 'Deeds, not words' quoted *The Mask of Anarchy*. Sylvia Pankhurst's East London Federation of Suffragettes worked closely with the No Conscription Fellowship, one of whose founders was Fenner Brockway. Olive Waterman, who joined as the ELFS as a girl of 13 in 1913, used to take food to the conscientious objectors hiding in Epping Forest during the First World War and accompanied Brockway to open air meetings for which she drummed up an audience by reciting Shelley and Blake. It is significant that the poems were familiar enough to attract working people. In America, young women garment workers in New York learnt Shelley's *Mask of Anarchy* and formed part of the 'Rising of the Twenty Thousand', the remarkable 1909 garment workers' strike.[8] Mahatma Gandhi, like George Bernard Shaw and others, was inspired by Shelley's vegetarianism. Gandhi was to adopt Shelley's non-violent approach to authority in his campaign against the Salt Tax in the 1920s.

The influence of Shelley on the American left continued, through such representative figures as W.E.B. du Bois and Ella Reeve Bloor. Theodor W. Adorno, Bertolt Brecht and Walter Benjamin admired and identified with him.[9] But his poetic reputation waned after attacks by T.S. Eliot and F.R. Leavis in the 1930s and by the New Critics in the United States – so much so that for 30 years even to 'mention Shelley' was to incur the stigma of having 'bad taste in literature'.[10] Yet Shelley's poetry never lost its popularity among WEA students or its position in, say, miners' libraries. Excellent and thorough studies such as those of Kenneth Cameron and Geoffrey Matthews began to rehabilitate Shelley's work in the 1950s. It started to become more popular in the 1960s among students and in 1969 Mick Jagger quoted *Adonais*, Shelley's elegy for Keats, at the Rolling Stones' free concert in Hyde Park in memory of fellow Stone, Brian Jones. Like Blake, Shelley became a counter-cultural figure, a perspective reflected in films such as Ken Russell's *Gothic* (1986) and Ivan Passer's *Haunted Summer* (1988). Scholars became interested in Shelley studies with significant contributions being made until by the end of the twentieth century two major editions of Shelley's poetry were being undertaken.

In 1980, Paul Foot's *Red Shelley* attracted attention on the left, and this continued with his almost annual meetings on Shelley at the Socialist Workers Party conference, Marxism. Benjamin Zephaniah has told me of the interest in Shelley taken by the Sandinistas in Nicaragua, and also of the groups of young black men he speaks to who call Shelley their brother. Chinese students chanted the last stanzas of *The Mask of Anarchy* in Tiananmen Square in 1989. 'We are Many, They Are Few' became the slogan of the Poll Tax campaigners in 1990 and has since been adopted by the Occupy Movement. I referred in the Prologue to the film *We Are Many*.

Shelley's Political Poetry and Plays

The Mask of Anarchy and *Ozymandias* are both well known, valuable and important poems to all who speak truth to power. Shelley knew that workers need the confidence to fight back against oppression. His lines about the sleepy lions rising up, shaking themselves and showing their strength were written to inspire. But these are not his only contribution. Political thought runs through nearly all Shelley's poetry. While a complete collection of Shelley's overtly political poems including those in the Esdaile Notebook would be welcome, this would not complete his legacy to the left. There are also his plays, which have not received the attention from the theatre which they deserve but which nevertheless have a performance history.

The Cenci was performed on the professional stage in 1922, with Beatrice played by no less an actor than Sybil Thorndike, one of the first Dames of the theatre and a left-winger who supported strikers in the 1926 General Strike. It was so successful that her company revived it two years later. It has been performed since in England and America. Berthold Goldschmidt and Havergal Brian based operas upon it but, apart from a 1959 production at the Old Vic, it has never become part of the mainstream theatre. *Hellas* was successfully adapted as a radio play by Judith Chernaik produced by John Theocaris in 1976, with Greek-style music by David Cain.[11] *Swellfoot the Tyrant*, perhaps the only play in which the 'swinish multitude' storms Parliament, has never been performed to my knowledge. *Prometheus Unbound* has been performed but would require a very high standard of production to do justice to the poetry and it might benefit from cutting to succeed on stage.

A Defence of Poetry

In 1821, Shelley's friend Peacock wrote an essay, *The Four Ages of Poetry*. Peacock's contention was that the standard of modern poetry was so low that poets ought to turn to the more 'useful' disciplines, economics and political economy. Shelley himself had said something similar when he told Peacock that poetry was 'very subordinate to moral & political science', but, in response to Peacock's essay, he defended poetry and poets as part of the imaginative life of humanity. He admits that there are bad poets, but that should not reflect on poetry itself. He linked his *Defence of Poetry* to politics when he recycled in it some of the passages from *A Philosophical View of Reform*. In doing so, Shelley did not limit poetry to the art of words but included imaginative and original thought.

Shelley pointed out that poetry – he included drama and certain prose writers under the heading – is found in every form of society, however primitive, together with music and the plastic arts. Poetry 'enlarges the circumference of the imagination by replenishing it'. Poetry inspires people with different ideas when tyranny has been triumphant; it delights both children and older people (p. 675). To ignore poetry is to ignore a basic need of human nature. Shelley suggested in *A Philosophical View* that the flourishing of art accompanies a struggle for liberation. He said that 'our own will be a memorable age in intellectual achievements, and we live among such philosophers and poets as surpass beyond comparison any who have appeared since the last struggle for civil and religious liberty', i.e. the English Revolution (p. 700) – modern critics would agree with the greatness of the Romantic poets. A similar flourishing of art and poetry took place around the Russian Revolution, and in the political awakening among young people in the 1960s and in Poland in the 1970s and 1980s.

Peacock argued that economics is more useful. Shelley responded that by lacking imagination the economists in modern England 'tend [. . .] to exasperate [aggravate] at once the extremes of luxury and want. [. . .] The rich have become richer, and the poor have become poorer, and the vessel of the state is driven between the Scylla and Charybdis of anarchy and despotism' (p. 694). 'From what other cause has it arisen that the discoveries which should have lightened, have added a weight to the curse imposed on Adam?' (p. 696) Adam is the worker. To ally yourself with these economists is to ally yourself with the modern successors of Dickens's Gradgrind who can only measure and calculate, and who have brought their system into every area of life: health, education, art.

Shelley did not undervalue the skills of the economist or political theorist, but said that we need the imagination to act on them. The people with the imagination are the artists of the human race, not its economists. It will be remembered that the economists he was thinking of were the architects of free market capitalism. In the twenty-first century we are seeing the effects of what they have built.

Cobbett's or Bentham's manifestos when read today seem quaint as they set out programmes for a former era based on society as it no longer is. *A Philosophical View* generalised the issues and looked forward to a society which we have not arrived at yet and so it is still relevant. Shelley reminds us that our goal is equality and that every campaign that brings us nearer is worth fighting. Although he saw little importance in tweaking the Parliamentary system, he saw immense gain in encouraging activity and learning about politics and achieving goals. Shelley did not expect reform without a strong movement outside Parliament, and he thought that people became stronger and more political through fighting for them, as the Greek he mentioned in the notes to *Hellas* had changed.[12] These are important lessons to those who think that the working class is not capable of fighting back, still less of governing.

Shelley believed that the leading reformers should have taken the advantage they had of massive support and desire for activity in 1819 instead of letting the mood peter out and supporters become discouraged and apathetic – as he put it 'sunk into incurable supineness'.[13] He also realised that extreme poverty, such as he had seen in Dublin, made people unable to think beyond survival. These are no less problems today. Shelley spoke of the oppression of the 'double aristocracy', the landowners and the bankers and stockbrokers. Today it is clearer than it was to him that they are the same class. They intermarry, share the same pursuits, and are richer than ever.

He saw the importance of a free press to oppose claims that it was 'sedition' to publish anything against the government, royalty and the Church. Such opposition is not illegal today, but the owners of newspapers and TV channels effectively censor what politics we read or see while presenting their own views. Meanwhile more and more laws are being introduced which echo those of 1817–19 in restricting our freedom. In the twenty-first century, it would not be possible for the 'swinish multitude' to get near enough to Parliament to storm it as the pigs did in *Swellfoot the Tyrant*.

Shelley's atheism is acceptable in Britain today, but while he claimed the right for himself not to believe in God, he supported the right of others to believe. He saw no reason why people of all religion and none should not live together amicably. It is an important lesson for today when attacks on belief can turn into attacks on minorities. Although he expressed unacceptable views about Jews and Italians, these were superficial reactions relying on 'national character' stereotypes which obtained in his own day. When discussing the political future, he was confident that these 'faults' would disappear.

In 2015, the national debt is even greater and has become a global debt. Inequality has reached the point where 80 people have wealth equal to the other billions, but the poor are again being forced to pay the interest on the debt while the rich are avoiding the taxes everyone else pays. Education has become narrower and is moving more and more out of reach of the poor.

A poet, for Shelley, was someone with imagination, foresight and sympathy, and these faculties are needed now just as much as they were 200 years ago. Shelley's *Defence* reminds us that science, *per se*, is not better or more useful than art, and that scientific knowledge must be used with imagination and vision. Discoveries cannot be allowed to serve only one section of the community. We need our visions for the future and our hopes to put them into practice. We need to be imaginative as well as practical, to remember when we are organising to allow room for poetry, new ideas and unexpected elements. There is a tendency to look for art in the wrong places such as West End theatre and official art galleries, yet new exciting art may be alongside us without our recognising it. Subsidies are increasingly given to 'centres of excellence' instead of local arts and community centres or touring theatre companies. It is no coincidence that funding for working people's art has been withdrawn or that one of the first cuts of Margaret Thatcher's 1979 government was the funding to political theatre companies. As Shelley wrote in 1821, art can be a political inspiration and should be at the forefront of political ideas.

Notes

Unless otherwise stated, quotations from Shelley's poetry and prose are taken from Oxford World Classics (*OWC*) edited by Zachary Leader and Michael O'Neill (Oxford, Oxford University Press, 2003).

CPPBS   *The Complete Poetry of Percy Bysshe Shelley,* edited by Donald H. Reiman and Neil Fraistat, 3 vols to date (Baltimore: Johns Hopkins University Press, 1999).

MWSJ   *The Journals of Mary Shelley, 1814–44*, edited by Paula R. Feldman and Diana Scott-Kilvert (Baltimore: The Johns Hopkins University Press, 1995).

MWSL/I   *The Letters of Mary Wollstonecraft Shelley*, 3 vols, I, edited by Betty T. Bennett (Baltimore: The Johns Hopkins University Press, 1980).

OWC   *Percy Bysshe Shelley, The Major Works*, edited by Zachary Leader and Michael O'Neill (Oxford: Oxford University Press, 2003).

PBSLI/II   *The Letters of Percy Bysshe Shelley*, edited by F.L. Jones, 2 vols (Oxford: Clarendon Press, 1964).

POS   *The Poems of Shelley*, edited by Kelvin Everest and Geoffrey Matthews, 4 vols (London: Longman, 1989).

PW   *Shelley: Poetical Works*, edited by Thomas Hutchinson, corr. by Geoffrey Matthews (Oxford: Oxford University Press, 1971).

PWPBS   *The Prose Works of Percy Bysshe Shelley Volume 1*, edited by E.B. Murray (Oxford: Clarendon Press, 1993).

SPP   *Shelley's Poetry and Prose*, edited by Donald H. Reiman and Neil Fraistat (New York: Norton, 2002).

Prologue

1. Peter Quennell (ed.) *Byron: A Self-Portrait in His Own Words* (Oxford: Oxford University Press, 1990), p. 717.
2. *PBSLI*, p. 314.
3. *MWSJ*, p. 195; *PBSLII*, p. 100.

Chapter 1

1. John Cordy Jeaffreson, *The Real Shelley* (London: Hurst and Blackett, 1885), pp. 24–5; also see Ian Gilmour, *The Making of the Poets: Byron and Shelley in Their Time* (London: Chatto, 2002).
2. Susan Cabell Djabri with Annabelle F. Hughes and Jeremy Knight, *The Shelleys of Field Place* (Horsham: Friends of Horsham Museum on behalf of Horsham Museum Society, 2003), pp. 3, 9–12, 59–68.
3. *PBSLI*, p. 239.
4. James Bieri, *Percy Bysshe Shelley, A Biography*, 2 vols (Newark: University of Delaware Press, 2004), I, p. 144; Thomas Medwin, *The Life of Percy Bysshe Shelley*, 2 vols (London: Thomas Cautley Newby, 1847), p. 11.
5. Djabri, *The Shelleys of Field Place*, p. 1; Ken Prichard-Jones, 'The Influence of Field Place and its Surroundings on Percy Bysshe Shelley', *Keats Shelley Review*, (1993–94), VIII, 132–50, p. 142; Paul O'Brien, *Shelley and Revolutionary Ireland* (London: Redwords, 2002), p. 102.
6. George Rudé, *Revolutionary Europe 1783–1815* (Glasgow: Collins, 1964), pp. 84–93.
7. Ibid., pp. 139–45, 172–4.
8. G.D.H. Cole and Raymond Postgate, *The Common People 1746–1938* (London: Methuen & Co., 1938), p. 142.
9. P.A. Brown, *The French Revolution in English History* (London: George Allen & Unwin, 1923), pp. 38, 69, 70, 72.
10. Ibid., p. 75.
11. Paul Foot, *The Vote: How it was Won and How it was Undermined* (London: Viking, 2005), p. 51.
12. Cole and Postgate, *Common People*, p. 114.
13. Brown, *The French Revolution*, p. 77; Fintan O'Toole, *A Traitor's Kiss* (London: Granta, 1997), p. 253.
14. M. Patterson, *Sir Francis Burdett and his Times*, 2 vols (London: Macmillan, 1931), I, pp. 67–78; Iain McCalman, *Radical Underworld* (Cambridge: Cambridge University Press, 1988), pp. 32–3.
15. Medwin, *The Life of Percy Bysshe Shelley*, I, p. 7.
16. Linda Kelly, *Richard Brinsley Sheridan* (London: Sinclair-Stevenson, 1997), p. 295.
17. Jim Smyth, *The Men of No Property* (London: Macmillan, 1992), p. 89; Peter Berresford Ellis, *A History of the Irish Working Class* (London: Pluto Press, 1985), p. 78.
18. Peter Fryer, *Staying Power* (London: Pluto Press, 1984), p. 36.

19. Ibid., pp. 68–71.
20. www.quaker.org.uk/quakers-and-abolition-slave-trade [accessed 16 February 2014]; Fryer, *Staying Power*, pp. 209–210; Brown, *The French Revolution*, p. 93.
21. Cole and Postgate, *The Common People*, pp. 87–91.
22. Jeremy Knight, *Horsham's History* (Horsham: Friends of Horsham Museum on behalf of Horsham Museum Society, 2006), pp. 31–32; Brown, *The French Revolution*, p. 93.
23. Susan Cabell Djabri and Jeremy Knight, *The Letters of Bysshe and Timothy Shelley* (Horsham: Friends of Horsham Museum on behalf of Horsham Museum Society, 2000), p. 63; Djabri, *The Shelleys of Field Place*, pp. 94–7, 106–12.
24. Cole and Postgate, *The Common People*, p. 57; Elie Halévy, *England in 1815* (London: Ernest Benn, 1949), p. 127.
25. Matthew Roberts, *Political Movements in Urban England 1832–1914* (Basingstoke: Palgrave Macmillan, 2009) pp. 14–15.
26. Brown, *The French Revolution*, pp. 10–25, 103.
27. Ibid., pp. 97–8, 102; Cole and Postgate, *The Common People*, pp. 150–1.
28. Matthew Roberts, *Political Movements in Urban England 1832–1914* (Basingstoke: Palgrave Macmillan, 2009), pp. 14–15; Brown, *The French Revolution*, pp. 112, 127.
29. William St Clair, *The Godwins and the Shelleys* (London: Faber & Faber, 1989), pp. 129–31.
30. Cole and Postgate, *The Common People*, p. 163; Brown, *The French Revolution*, pp. 151–2.
31. Djabri, *The Shelleys of Field Place*, p. 130; Kenneth Neill Cameron, *The Young Shelley* (London: Victor Gollancz, 1951), p. 46.
32. Djabri, *The Shelleys of Field Place*, pp. 102–3.
33. Humbert Wolfe (ed.), *The Life of Percy Bysshe Shelley*, 2 vols (London: J.M. Dent, 1933), I, p. 23.
34. Edward Dowden, *The Life of Percy Bysshe Shelley*, 2 vols (London: Kegan Paul, Trench & Co., 1886), I, p. 78.
35. Bieri, *Percy Bysshe Shelley*, p. 144.
36. Prichard-Jones, 'The Influence of Field Place', p. 137; Wolfe, *The Life of Percy Bysshe Shelley*, I, p. 22.
37. Wolfe, *The Life of Percy Bysshe Shelley*, I, pp. 22–4; *PBSLI*, p. 87.
38. Ibid., pp. 24–8; *PBSLI*, p. 1.
39. Medwin, *The Life of Percy Bysshe Shelley*, I, pp. 15–17.

40. Dowden, *The Life of Percy Bysshe Shelley*, I, p. 16n.

41. Medwin, *The Life of Percy Bysshe Shelley*, I, pp. 33–4.

42. Ibid., pp. 23, 35–6, 52.

43. Newman Ivey White, *Shelley*, 2 vols (London: Secker & Warburg, 1947), I, pp. 34–6.

44. Angus Graham-Campbell, 'Some Notes on Shelley's Eton Days', *Keats Shelley Review*, VIII (1993–1994), 151–7, pp. 151–3; Illustrations with explanatory captions: 158–61.

45. Medwin, *The Life of Percy Bysshe Shelley*, I, p. 363.

46. Wolfe, *The Life of Percy Bysshe Shelley*, I, p. 84.

47. Dowden, *The Life of Percy Bysshe Shelley*, I, pp. 26n, 28, 35.

48. Nora Crook and Derek Guiton, *Shelley's Venomed Melody* (Cambridge: Cambridge University Press, 1986), pp. 21–22; Medwin, *The Life of Percy Bysshe Shelley*, I, p. 52.

49. Wolfe, *The Life of Percy Bysshe Shelley*, I, p. 23; *PBSLI*, pp. 2–5; *PBSLII*, p. 169; Medwin, *The Life of Percy Bysshe Shelley*, I, p. 110.

50. Djabri, *The Shelleys of Field Place*, p. 106; Knight, *Horsham's History*, pp. 34–36.

51. Thompson, *The Making of the English Working Class*, p. 84; Cole and Postgate, *The Common People*, p. 177; Cameron, *The Young Shelley*, p. 48.

52. *CPPBS*, I, p. 43.

53. Medwin, *The Life of Percy Bysshe Shelley*, I, p. 67; *PBSLI*, p. 6

54. Djabri, *The Shelleys of Field Place*, p. 108; Cameron, *The Young Shelley*, p. 330.

55. Wolfe, *The Life of Percy Bysshe Shelley*, I, pp. 26, 27.

56. Martin Priestman, *Romantic Atheism* (Cambridge: Cambridge University Press, 1999), pp. 2–5, 14–18, 184; Medwin, *The Life of Percy Bysshe Shelley*, I, p. 11.

57. Wolfe, *The Life of Percy Bysshe Shelley*, II, pp. 154–5.

58. Desmond Hawkins, *Shelley's First Love* (London: Kyle Cathie, 1992), pp. 34–43.

59. Wolfe, *The Life of Percy Bysshe Shelley*, II, p. 155; Wolfe, *The Life of Percy Bysshe Shelley*, I, p. 28.

60. Hawkins, *Shelley's First Love*, pp. 47 (ll.12–30), 49, 103.

61. Wolfe, *The Life of Percy Bysshe Shelley*, I, p. 129; William Godwin, *An Enquiry Concerning Political Justice* Vol III, Mark Philp (ed.), *Political and Philosophical Writings of William Godwin* (London, William Pickering, 1993), p. 326.

62. Denis Florence MacCarthy, *Shelley's Early Life* (London: J.C. Hotten, 1872), p. 95.
63. White, *Shelley*, I, pp. 70–6.
64. Wolfe, *The Life of Percy Bysshe Shelley*, I, p. 155; Medwin, *The Life of Percy Bysshe Shelley*, I, p. 146.
65. O'Brien, *Shelley and Revolutionary Ireland*, pp. 28–30; MacCarthy, *Shelley's Early Life*, pp. 256–7; O'Toole, *A Traitor's Kiss*, p. 420.
66. O'Toole, *A Traitor's Kiss*, p. 420; Cameron, *The Young Shelley*, pp. 49–50.
67. MacCarthy, *Shelley's Early Life*, pp. 93, 96, 25–7; the poem was re-discovered in 2006 but the owners will not allow it to be published, although it was exhibited at the 2010 Bodleian Library 'Shelley's Ghost' exhibition; http://michaelrosenblog.blogspot.co.uk/2013/07/shelleys-revolutionary-poem-hidden-away.html.
68. Wolfe, *The Life of Percy Bysshe Shelley*, I, pp. 133, 82–4.
69. Ibid., p. 84; *PBSLI*, p. 19.
70. *CPPBS*, I, p. 236.
71. Wolfe, *The Life of Percy Bysshe Shelley*, I, p. 84.
72. White, *Shelley*, I, p. 94.
73. Wolfe, *The Life of Percy Bysshe Shelley*, I, p. 28; *PBSLI*, p. 48.
74. *PBSLI*, pp. 27–29, 35; Cameron, *The Young Shelley*, p. 330.
75. Wolfe, *The Life of Percy Bysshe Shelley*, I, pp. 160, 164.
76. Priestman, *Romantic Atheism*, p. 184.
77. *PBSLI*, p. 52.
78. *PBSLI*, pp. 54, 264; O'Brien, *Shelley and Revolutionary Ireland*, p. 99.
79. *PWPBS*, pp. 3–5.
80. Cameron, *The Young Shelley*, pp. 328–30.
81. *PBSLI*, p. 228.
82. Wolfe, *The Life of Percy Bysshe Shelley*, I, pp. 168–72; Bieri, *Percy Bysshe Shelley*, I, pp. 159–60.
83. Hawkins, *Shelley's First Love*, p. 83.
84. *PBSLI*, pp. 74, 57n, 209n, 368n.; White, *Shelley*, I, p. 115.
85. Wolfe, *The Life of Percy Bysshe Shelley*, I, pp. 169, 42.
86. White, *Shelley*, I, pp. 115–16.

Chapter 2

1. *PBSLI*, p. 57n.
2. Newman Ivey White, *Shelley*, 2 vols (London: Secker & Warburg, 1947), I, pp. 122–5; *PBSLI*, p. 60, 60n.

3. Kenneth Neill Cameron, *The Young Shelley* (London: Victor Gollancz, 1951), p. 84; *PBSLI*, p. 74.
4. *PBSLI*, p. 230.
5. Humbert Wolfe (ed.), *The Life of Percy Bysshe Shelley*, 2 vols (London: J.M. Dent, 1933), I, p. 181.
6. Wolfe, *The Life of Percy Bysshe Shelley*, I, p. 156; *PBSLI*, p. 149.
7. George Rudé, *Revolutionary Europe 1783–1815* (Glasgow: Collins, 1964), pp. 265–8; *PBSLI*, p. 208.
8. See Nora Crook and Derek Guiton, *Shelley's Venomed Melody* (Cambridge: Cambridge University Press, 1986) for a full discussion of this subject.
9. Sharon Ruston, *Shelley and Vitality* (Basingstoke: Palgrave Macmillan, 2005), pp. 80–2; Elie Halévy, *England in 1815* (London: Ernest Benn, 1949), p. 553.
10. Ruston, *Shelley and Vitality*, pp. 41–2.
11. Ibid., pp. 46–72.
12. Ibid., pp. 85–6, 9, 21–2.
13. Edward John Trelawny, *Records of Shelley, Byron and the Author* (Harmondsworth: Penguin, 1973), p. 63; Crook and Guiton, *Shelley's Venomed Melody*, pp. 1–2.
14. William Godwin, *An Enquiry Concerning Political Justice Vol III*, Mark Philp (ed.), *Political and Philosophical Writings of William Godwin* (London, William Pickering, 1993), pp. 250, 260–3.
15. Thomas Paine, *Rights of Man* (Harmondsworth: Penguin, 1984), pp. 82–3.
16. James Bieri, *Percy Bysshe Shelley, A Biography* 2 vols (Newark: University of Delaware Press, 2004), I, pp. 180–1.
17. *PBSLI*, p. 62.
18. Ibid., pp. 65n, 66n.
19. Cameron, *The Young Shelley*, pp. 84–5; Bieri, *Percy Bysshe Shelley*, I, p. 37.
20. *PBSLI*, p. 166n.
21. Ibid., p. 127; Cameron, *The Young Shelley*, p. 169.
22. Wolfe, *The Life of Percy Bysshe Shelley*, I, p. 32.
23. Cameron, *The Young Shelley*, pp. 89, 335.
24. *PBSLI*, p. 71.
25. Cameron, *The Young Shelley*, p. 91; White, *Shelley*, I, p. 134; *PBSLI*, p. 105n.
26. Wolfe, *The Life of Percy Bysshe Shelley*, I, p. 156.
27. *PBSLI*, p. 158; Cameron, *The Young Shelley*, p. 45.

28. Wolfe, *The Life of Percy Bysshe Shelley*, I, p. 197.

29. en.wikisource.org/wiki/Dictionary_of_National_Biography,_1885–1900; http://hansard.millbanksystems.com/commons/1810/feb/21/breach-of-privilege-mr-john-gale-jones [accessed 6 February 2015].

30. M. Patterson, *Sir Francis Burdett and His Times*, 2 vols (London: Macmillan, 1931), I, pp. 242–50; Iain McCalman, *Radical Underworld* (Cambridge: Cambridge University Press, 1988), p. 89.

31. George Rudé, *The Crowd in History* (New York: John Wiley & Sons, 1964), p. 80.

32. Ian Haywood, *Romanticism and Caricature* (Cambridge: Cambridge University Press, 2013), pp. 33, 38.

33. G.D.H. Cole and Raymond Postgate, *The Common People 1746–1938* (Methuen & Co, 1938), pp. 143–4; J.L. Hammond and Barbara Hammond, *The Skilled Labourer* (Abingdon: Alan Sutton Publishing, 1995), p. 83.

34. Wolfe, *The Life of Percy Bysshe Shelley*, I, pp. 157–8.

35. *PBSLI*, pp. 105–106; *CPPBS*, I, p. 449.

36. *PBSLI*, pp. 110, 221.

37. Ibid., pp. 113–14, 123–4.

38. Ibid., pp. 85.

39. Ibid., p. 151.

40. Ibid., pp. 120, 135.

41. Ibid., pp. 117–119, 137n.

42. Ibid., pp. 81, 135, 184, 194.

43. William Godwin, *An Enquiry Concerning Political Justice* Vol III, Mark Philp (ed.), *Political and Philosophical Writings of William Godwin* (London, William Pickering, 1993), pp. 453–4.

44. I am grateful to Nicola Lloyd for information about Charlotte Dacre.

45. https://sites.google.com/site/maryjanesdaughter/home/claire-s-father/sir-john-lethbridge [accessed 1 February 2015].

46. *PBSLI*, p. 122n; Percy Bysshe Shelley, *Zastrozzi and St. Irvyne*, Stephen Behrendt (ed.) (Oxford: Oxford University Press, 1986), p. 197.

47. Wolfe, *The Life of Percy Bysshe Shelley*, I, p. 32; *PBSLI*, pp. 71, 163.

48. 'Note to *Queen Mab*', *OWC*, pp. 10–20; *PBSLI*, p. 152.

49. *PBSLI*, pp. 165n, 67.

50. Ibid., pp. 155, 166n.

51. Ibid., pp. 175–80, 203.

52. Ibid., p. 122 .

53. Ibid., pp. 119, 232, 240.

54. Quoted in Crook and Guiton, *Shelley's Venomed Melody*, p. 107.

55. *PBSLI*, pp. 159, 159n.

56. See White, *Shelley*, I, pp. 274–5, for a summary of financial matters.

57. *PBSLI*, p. 212.

58. Ibid., pp. 219–21, 223.

59. Ian Birchall, *The Spectre of Babeuf* (Basingstoke: Macmillan, 1997), pp. 64–5, 85–7, 168.

60. www.rc.umd.edu/editions/southey_letters/Part_One/HTML/letterEEd. 26.222.html; www.rc.umd.edu/editions/southey_letters/Part_Two/ HTML/letterEEd.26.477.html [accessed 20 March 2015].

61. Stuart Andrews, *Robert Southey, History, Politics, Religion* (Basingstoke: Palgrave Macmillan, 2011), p. 22; *PBSLI*, p. 227.

62. Cole and Postgate, *The Common People*, pp. 39–40.

63. *PBSLI*, p. 223.

64. Michael Scrivener, *Radical Shelley* (Princeton: Princeton University Press, 1982), p. 53; workers' stories quoted in Paul Mason, *Live Working or Die Fighting* (London: Harvill Secker, 2007), pp. 14–15; E.P. Thompson, *The Making of the English Working Class* (Harmondsworth, Penguin, 1980), pp. 599, 599n.

65. Cole and Postgate, *Common People*, p. 172.

66. Hammond and Hammond, *The Skilled Labourer*, pp. 58–72; Halévy, *England in 1815*, pp. 242–7, 292, 326–30.

67. Rudé, *The Crowd in History*, p. 81; Cole and Postgate, *Common People*, pp. 180–4; Thompson, *The Making of the English Working Class*, pp. 572–89.

68. Rudé, *The Crowd in History*, pp. 81–6; *PBSLI*, p. 213.

69. Cole and Postgate, *Common People*, pp. 182–4; Thompson, *The Making of the English Working Class*, p. 598.

70. Cole and Postgate, *Common People*, p. 181; *PBSLI*, p. 351n.

71. Jim Smyth, *The Men of No Property* (London: Macmillan, 1992), pp. 10–11, 30–1.

72. Robert Kee, *The Green Flag*, 3 vols, 'The Most Distressful Country' (London: Quartet, 1976), I, pp. 22–23; Peter Berresford Ellis, *A History of the Irish Working Class*, (London: Pluto Press, 1985), p. 54.

73. Smyth, *The Men of No Property*, pp. 20–25, 54–60; Halévy, *England in 1815*, p. 208.

74. Berresford Ellis, *A History of the Irish Working Class*, pp. 71–2.

75. Smyth, *The Men of No Property*, pp. 92–3, 97; Grainne Yeats, *The Belfast Harp Festival* (Dublin: Gael Linn, 1992).

76. O'Brien, *Shelley and Revolutionary Ireland*, pp. 62–3; Kee, *The Green Flag*, I, p. 67.

77. Frank Harte and Donal Lunny, *1798: The First Year of Liberty* (Dublin: Hummingbird Records), track 17.

78. Kee, *The Green Flag*, I, pp. 87–8.

79. Thomas Pakenham, *The Year of Liberty* (London: Orion Books, 1992), pp. 45, 71, 100–3, 245–60.

80. Ibid., pp. 187–193.

81. Ibid., pp. 344–6.

82. Ibid., pp. 232, 242–3.

83. O'Brien, *Shelley and Revolutionary Ireland*, pp. 72–3, 82–4.

84. Dowden Edward, *The Life of Percy Bysshe Shelley,* 2 vols (London: Kegan Paul, Trench & Co., 1886), I, p. 240.

85. Sean O'Faolain, *King of the Beggars* (London: Thomas Nelson and Sons, 1938), pp. 133, 137.

86. *PBSLI*, pp. 234, 235.

87. O'Brien, *Shelley and Revolutionary Ireland*, p. 76.

88. P.M.S. Dawson, *The Unacknowledged Legislator* (Oxford: Clarendon Press, 1980), p. 18.

89. *PBSLI*, p. 267.

90. Ibid., p. 263.

91. Ibid., pp. 270–271.

92. Ibid., pp. 255, 278.

93. Page numbers for the *Address* and the *Proposals* from *PWPBS*.

94. O'Brien, *Shelley and Revolutionary Ireland*, p. 104; PBSLI, p. 239.

95. O'Brien, *Shelley and Revolutionary Ireland*, p. 80; PBSLI, p. 264.

96. *PBSLI*, p. 265.

97. O'Brien, *Shelley and Revolutionary Ireland*, pp. 116–19, 133; *PBSLI*, pp. 255, 322.

98. O'Brien, *Shelley and Revolutionary Ireland*, pp. 120–1.

99. O'Faolain, *King of the Beggars*, pp. 74–81.

100. Cameron, *The Young Shelley*, pp. 145–7; *PBSLI*, p. 275; *PWPBS*, Appendix I, pp. 291–301.

101. *PBSLI*, pp. 267, 270n.

102. O'Faolain, *King of the Beggars*, pp. 358–64; O'Brien, *Shelley and Revolutionary Ireland*, p. 99.

103. *PBSLI*, p. 264.

104. White, *Shelley*, I, p. 227; Cameron, *The Young Shelley*, p. 169.

105. White, *Shelley*, I, pp. 228, 237; information about accommodation from owners of Shelley's Cottage Hotel (1992).
106. Thompson, *The Making of the English Working Class*, p. 623; H.M. Dowling, 'The Attack at Tanyrallt', *Keats-Shelley Memorial Bulletin*, XII (1961), 28–36, p. 31.
107. Thompson, *The Making of the English Working Class*, pp. 666–8.
108. Cameron, *The Young Shelley*, pp. 203–204.
109. Thompson, *The Making of the English Working Class*, p. 662.
110. *PWPBS*, p. 73.
111. Cameron, *The Young Shelley*, pp. 171–2; White, *Shelley*, I, p. 248.
112. White, *Shelley*, I, pp. 249–51; Cameron, *The Young Shelley*, pp. 175–9.

Chapter 3

1. Kenneth Neill Cameron, *The Young Shelley* (London: Victor Gollancz, 1951), p. 187.
2. Elisabeth Beazley, *Madocks and the Wonder of Wales* (London: Faber and Faber, 1967), pp. 57–8, 82–91, 99–156.
3. http://godwindiary.bodleian.ox.ac.uk [accessed 3 October, 2014]; Newman Ivey White, *Shelley*, 2 vols (London: Secker & Warburg, 1947), I, pp. 253–8.
4. Edward Baldwin, *Fables Ancient and Modern adapted for the Use of Children*, 2 vols (London: Thomas Hodgkins, 1805), I; Brian Alderson, '"Mister Gobwin" and His "Interesting Little Books, Adorned with Beautiful Copper-Plates"', *Princeton University Library Chronicle*, LIX, 2 (winter 1998), 159–91, pp. 163–6, 177–9. I am grateful to Brian Alderson for further information about the Godwins and for showing me some of their publications. The fables are also now available at www.rc.umd.edu/editions/godwin_fables/index/html.
5. *PBSLI*, p. 245.
6. *PBSLI*, pp. 331n, 336, 320n.
7. Beazley, *Madocks and the Wonder of Wales*, p. 18.
8. *PBSLI*, p. 356m; H.M. Dowling, 'The Attack at Tanyrallt', *Keats-Shelley Memorial Bulletin*, XII (1961), p. 32.
9. *PBSLI*, p. 258n.
10. Bieri James, *Percy Bysshe Shelley, A Biography*, 2 vols (Newark: University of Delaware Press, 2004), I, p. 273; White, *Shelley*, I, pp. 267–8.
11. *PBSLI*, pp. 340, 354.
12. Ibid., pp. 350, 351.

13. Ibid., pp. 355–6n; Dowling, 'The Attack at Tanyrallt', p. 35.

14. Richard Holmes, *Shelley: The Pursuit* (Harmondsworth: Penguin, 1987), p. 214; Dowden Edward, *The Life of Percy Bysshe Shelley,* 2 vols (London: Kegan Paul, Trench & Co., 1886), I, p. 357, 357n.

15. Cameron, *The Young Shelley*, p. 211.

16. Dowling, 'The Attack at Tanyrallt', p. 34.

17. White, *Shelley*, I, p. 193.

18. Michael Scrivener, *Radical Shelley* (Princeton: Princeton University Press, 1982), p. 58; Cameron, *The Young Shelley*, p. 175.

19. *PBSLI*, p. 566; letter from Eliza Westbrook to John Williams quoted in Holmes, *Shelley*, p. 197.

20. George Rudé, *Revolutionary Europe 1783–1815* (Glasgow: Collins, 1964), pp. 277–9; Elie Halévy, *England in 1815* (London: Ernest Benn, 1949), p. 99.

21. *PBSLI*, pp. 346, 376–7; White, *Shelley*, I, pp. 320–2.

22. *PW*, pp. 828–34, 832, 832n.

23. Mary Shelley, 'Notes on *Queen Mab*', *PW*, p. 837; *PBSLI*, pp. 274–5.

24. White, *Shelley*, I, pp. 325–32; Cameron, *The Young Shelley*, pp. 219–21.

25. *PBSLI*, p. 384; Humbert Wolfe (ed.), *The Life of Percy Bysshe Shelley,* 2 vols (London: J.M. Dent, 1933), II, p. 323; I am grateful to Sarah Cox for information on the widespread popularity of breastfeeding.

26. *PBSLI*, p. 372n.

27. *PWPBS*, pp. 94, 123.

28. *PBSLI*, p. 403; White, *Shelley*, I, pp. 335–8.

29. *PBSLI*, pp. 389–90.

30. *PBSLI*, pp. 421n, 424n.

31. *PBLSI*, p. 414.

32. Wolfe, *The Life of Percy Bysshe Shelley*, II, p. 336; *PBSLI*, p. 421n.

33. Bieri, *Percy Bysshe Shelley*, pp. 349–52; *MWSJ*, p. 25.

34. *PBSLI*, p. 391; *MWSJ*, pp. 10, 13, 24–5.

35. *MWSJ*, pp. 49, 105; *MWSL*, pp. 6–11.

36. *The Journals of Claire Clairmont* ed. by Marion Kingston Stocking (Cambridge, MA: Harvard University Press, 1968), pp. 68, 250n.

37. Holmes, *Shelley*, pp. 293–4.

38. Marilyn Butler, *Romantics, Rebels and Reactionaries* (Oxford: Oxford University Press, 1982), p. 140; Michael O'Neill, *Shelley: A Literary Life* (Basingstoke: Palgrave Macmillan, 1989), pp. 56–8.

39. W.G. Bebbington, 'Shelley's Quaker Friend, Dr. Robert Pope', *KSMB*, V (1953) pp. 45–8; John Punshon, *Portrait in Grey* (London: Quaker Home Service, 1984), pp. 133–5, 155.

40. Mary Shelley, 'Note on the Revolt of Islam' in *PW*, p. 156; *PBSLI*, I, pp. 70–1.

41. Malcolm Chase, *The People's Farm* (Oxford: Clarendon Press, 1988), pp. 21–3; Alastair Bonnett, 'The Other Rights of Man', in *History Today*, September 2007, 42–5; E.P. Thompson, *The Making of the English Working Class* (Harmondsworth, Penguin, 1980), pp. 673–4; *MWSJ*, pp. 63–64; McCalman Iain, *Radical Underworld* (Cambridge: Cambridge University Press, 1988), pp. 21–4, 80–2, 92, 99–104; http://www.ditext. com/spence/rights.html; [accessed 17 January 2015].

42. A.H. Beavan, *James and Horace Smith* (London: Hurst and Blackett, 1899), pp. 302–3, 151; quoted in Bieri, II, p. 33.

43. Ibid., pp. 137–8; *MWSL*, p. 27.

44. John Belchem, *'Orator' Hunt* (Oxford: Clarendon Press, 1985), p. 22.

45. Roger Ingpen, *Shelley in England* (London: Kegan Paul, Trench, Trubner & Co, 1917), pp. 456–8; *MWSJ*, p. 77n.

46. *PBLSI*, pp. 525, 547.

47. Mary Shelley, 'Note on The Revolt of Islam', *PW*, p. 157; *MWSL*, p. 29.

48. *PWPBS*, p. 280.

49. Thompson, *The Making of the English Working Class*, pp. 282–3, 294n; J.L. Hammond and Barbara Hammond, *The Skilled Labourer* (Abingdon: Alan Sutton Publishing, 1995), pp. 94–5; G.D.H. Cole and Raymond Postgate, *The Common People 1746–1938* (Methuen & Co, 1938), pp. 205–6; Halévy, *England in 1815*, pp. 219, 246, 250.

50. James Grande, *William Cobbett, the Press and Rural England*, (Basingstoke: Palgrave Macmillan, 2014), pp. 23–6, 64.

51. *PW*, p. 157; *The Clairmont Correspondence*, Marion Kingston Stocking (ed.) (Baltimore: Johns Hopkins Univeristy Press, 1995), p. 91.

52. Cole and Postgate, *The Common People*, p. 207.

53. Thompson, *The Making of the English Working Class*, pp. 694–6; Cole and Postgate, *The Common People*, pp. 215–16.

54. Thompson, *The Making of the English Working Class*, pp. 697–9; Belchem, 'Orator' Hunt, pp. 58–68.

55. Kenneth Cameron, 'Shelley and the Reformers', *English Literary History*, 12, No. 1 (Mar. 1945), 62–85, p. 71; *PWPBS*, pp. 171–4.

56. Karl Marx and Frederick Engels, *Manifesto of the Communist Party*, Andy Blunden (ed.), Marxists Internet Archive (2010), p. 62.

57. M. Patterson, *Sir Francis Burdett and his Times*, 2 vols (London: Macmillan, 1931), II, p. 457; *PWPBS*, pp. 175, 517.

58. Quoted in G.D.H. Cole, *The Life of Robert Owen* (London: Macmillan, 1939), p. 16; http://godwindiary.bodleian.ox.ac.uk [accessed 3 October, 2014].

59. Cole and Postgate, *The Common People*, pp. 216–8; Thompson, *The Making of the English Working Class*, pp. 723–32; William Cobbett, *Political Register*, 23 May 1818, pp. 580–1; McCalman, *Radical Underworld*, p. 83.

60. *OWC*, pp. 624–5.

61. Ibid., p. 630.

62. Shelley's background reading for this poem included works on the French Revolution. Nora Crook informs me that an unpublished booklist in the Pforzheimer Collection, New York Public Library, shows that this reading was wider than has been supposed.

63. *CPPBS*, III, pp. 564, 572–3.

64. Wolfe, *The Life of Percy Bysshe Shelley*, II, p. 323; Nora Crook and Stephen Allen, 'The Marlow Expurgation: New light on the revision of Shelley's most scandalous poem', *Times Literary Supplement*, 22 February 2013.

65. *PBSLI*, p. 577.

66. *MWSLI*, pp. 52–4.

67. Ibid., p. 43.

Chapter 4

1. George Rudé, *Revolutionary Europe 1783–1815* (Glasgow: Collins, 1964), pp. 207, 213.

2. Lucy Riall, *Risorgimento* (Basingstoke: Palgrave Macmillan, 2009), pp. 5–9; Alexander Grab 'From the French Revolution to Napoleon' in *Italy in the Nineteenth Century*, John A. Davis (ed.) (Oxford: Oxford University Press, 2000), pp. 26–34.

3. Riall, *Risorgimento*, pp. 10–14; Grab, 'From the French Revolution to Napoleon', p. 48; David Laven, 'The Age of Restoration', in Davis, *Italy*, pp. 53–8.

4. Arnold Anthony Schmidt, *Byron and the Rhetoric of Italian Nationalism* (Basingstoke: Palgrave Macmillan, 2010), p. 25.

5. *PBSLII*, pp. 114, 69, 22.

6. Ibid., p. 24n.

7. Ibid., pp. 32, 36–38.

8. Ibid., p. 41; *MWSJ*, pp. 206n, 224–7; *MWSL/I*, p. 46.

9. *MWSL/I*, p. 83.

10. James Bieri, *Percy Bysshe Shelley, A Biography*, 2 vols (Newark: University of Delaware Press, 2005), II, pp. 367n, 35; Peter Quennell (ed.) *Byron: A Self-Portrait in His Own Words* (Oxford: Oxford University Press, 1990), pp. 526, 689, 717.

11. Rudé, *Revolutionary Europe*, p. 219.

12. Nora Crook and Derek Guiton, *Shelley's Venomed Melody* (Cambridge University Press, 1986), pp. 110–114; *PW*, p. 30.

13. Davis, *Italy*, p. 48; Riall, *Risorgimento*, p. 93; *PBSLII*, p. 211.

14. G.M. Matthews, 'A Volcano's Voice in Shelley', *SPP*, p. 563; Paul Foot, *Red Shelley* (London: Bookmarks, 1984), p. 194.

15. *Prometheus Unbound*, *POS*, pp. 457–60, pp. 471–649.

16. *PBSLII*, pp. 174, 127, 94.

17. Ibid., pp. 108.

18. John Gardner, *Poetry and Political Protest* (Basingstoke: Palgrave Macmillan, 2011), p. 224.

19. *PBSLII*, pp. 377n, 196.

20. Ibid., pp. 92, 94.

21. Ibid., pp. 102–03.

22. Ibid., p. 178.

23. I am grateful to Nora Crook for suggesting this.

24. *PBSLII*, p. 190n.

25. Ibid., p. 97; *MWSJ*, p. 252n; *MWSL/I*, p. 103.

26. *POS*, p. 709; *PBSLII*, p. 109.

27. *PBSLII*, p. 115; *PW*, p. 335.

28. E.P. Thompson, *The Making of the English Working Class* (Harmondsworth, Penguin, 1980), pp. 698–707; *PBSLII*, p. 99.

29. *PBSLII*, p. 94.

30. PBSL/II, p. 115; Thompson, *The Making of the English Working Class*, p. 671.

31. Thompson, *The Making of the English Working Class*, pp. 706–07; John Belchem, *'Orator' Hunt* (Oxford: Clarendon Press, 1985), pp. 91–9.

32. R.J. White, *Waterloo to Peterloo* (London: Heinemann, 1957), p. 181.

33. George Swift's account transcribed by Chris Whitehead in *Return to Peterloo*, Robert Poole (ed.), *Manchester Region History Review*, 23 (2012), p. 146; Carlile's eyewitness account differs in detail from these, http://spartacus-educational.com/PRrepublican.htm [accessed 6 March 2015].

34. Thompson, *The Making of the English Working Class*, pp. 751–4.

35. *PBSLII*, pp. 119–20.

36. Ian Haywood, *Romanticism and Caricature* (Cambridge: Cambridge University Press, 2013), p. 94; Sidmouth wanted to counter the growth of Methodism, which he described as 'a Jacobin in the extreme', McCalman Iain, *Radical Underworld* (Cambridge: Cambridge University Press, 1988), p. 51.

37. Gardner, *Poetry and Political Protest*, pp. 71, 91; Rudé, *Revolutionary Europe*, p. 93.

38. Paul Foot, *The Vote: How it was Won and How it was Undermined* (London: Viking, 2005), p. 62.

39. Gardner, *Poetry and Political Protest*, p. 48; Thompson, *The Making of the English Working Class*, pp. 742–3.

40. Thompson, *The Making of the English Working Class*, pp. 755–6; M. Patterson, *Sir Francis Burdett and his Times*, 2 vols (London: Macmillan, 1931), II, p. 502.

41. Belchem, *'Orator' Hunt*, pp. 116–17, 125–6; Nicholas Roe, *John Keats and the Culture of Dissent* (Oxford: Clarendon Press, 1997), p. 253.

42. Thompson, *The Making of the English Working Class*, pp. 765–6.

43. Patterson, *Sir Francis Burdett and his Times*, II, pp. 496–7.

44. *PBSLII*, pp. 136–48.

45. *PBSLII*, p. 181; Kenneth Cameron, 'Shelley and the Reformers', *English Literary History*, 12, No. 1 (March 1945), p. 77, n61.

46. *PBSLII*, pp. 164, 201.

47. Christopher Goulding, *The Review of English Studies, New series*, 52, 206 (2001), pp. 233–7. I am grateful to Nora Crook for alerting me to this article.

48. Cameron, 'Shelley and the Reformers', p. 73n.

49. *PBSLII*, pp. 70–1.

50. *PBSLII*, p. 71n.

51. Elie Halévy, *England in 1815* (London: Ernest Benn, 1949), pp. 349, 358.

52. Malthus had suggested that the poor laws encouraged people to start families because they would not be afraid of starving to death, a measure of population control he thought had worked in more primitive societies. www.esp.org/books/malthus/population/malthus.pdf [accessed 7 January 2015].

53. http://oll.libertyfund.org/pages/1793-french-republic-constitution-of-1793 [accessed 8 January 2015].

54. G.D.H. Cole and Raymond Postgate, *The Common People 1746–1938* (London: Methuen & Co, 1938), p. 91.

55. *MWSLI*, p. 49.
56. Gardner, *Poetry and Political Protest*, p. 58.

Chapter 5

1. *PBSLII*, p. 207.
2. In 1979, Journeyman Press published a selection of these together with Eleanor Marx and Edward Aveling's 1888 lecture on Shelley; in 1990 Redwords published a slightly different selection with *A Philosophical View of Reform* introduced by Paul Foot.
3. *PBSLII*, p. 24n.
4. John Gardner, 'William Cobbett the Spy?' *Romanticism*, 18.1 (2012) 30–40.
5. *PBSLII*, pp. 151, 211.
6. Elie Halévy, *England in 1815* (London: Ernest Benn, 1949), p. 307.
7. *PBSLII*, p. 217.
8. Ibid., p. 223.
9. Ibid., p. 234.
10. Ibid., p. 266.
11. Arnold Anthony Schmidt, *Byron and the Rhetoric of Italian Nationalism* (Basingstoke: Palgrave Macmillan, 2010), pp. 38–42.
12. *PW*, p. 410.
13. *PBSLII*, p. 207.
14. Iain McCalman, *Radical Underworld* (Cambridge: Cambridge University Press, 1988), pp. 162–72, 176; John Gardner, *Poetry and Political Protest* (Basingstoke: Palgrave Macmillan, 2011), pp. 189–91; www.npg.org.uk/collections/search/set/86/Caricatures + against + Queen + Caroline [accessed 18 January 2015].
15. Gardner, *Poetry and Political Protest*, p. 198.
16. *PWPBS*, p. 280.
17. Nora Crook, 'Shelley's Jewish "Orations"', *Keats Shelley Journal* 59 (2010) 43–64.
18. Robert Kee, *The Green Flag*, 3 vols (London: Quartet, 1976), I, p. 158.
19. A.H. Beavan, *James and Horace Smith* (London: Hurst and Blackett, 1899), p. 176; for more on the Society for the Suppression of Vice, see Gardner, *Poetry and Political Protest*, p. 231n.
20. For more on Swellfoot and performance, see Jacqueline Mulhallen, *The Theatre of Shelley* (Cambridge: Openbooks, 2010), pp. 230–4.
21. *MWSLI*, p. 165.

22. *MWSLI*, pp. 183, 185.
23. Roderick Beaton, *Byron's War* (Cambridge: Cambridge University Press, 2013), p. 73.
24. William St Clair, *That Greece Might Still be Free* (Cambridge: Open Book Publishers, 2008), pp. 1, 6–8, 12, 31.
25. *PBSLII*, p. 368; Beaton, *Byron's War*, p. 287 n53.
26. Aristophanes, *The Frogs*, in *The Wasps, The Poet and the Women, The Frogs*, trans. by David Barrett (Harmondsworth: Penguin, 1964), ll. 1026–7.
27. Aeschylus, *The Persians*, ll. 243, ed. by Seth E. Bernadete in *Aeschylus* II (Chicago: Chicago University Press, 1956).
28. *PBSLII*, p. 365.
29. *PBSLI*, p. 257.
30. *PBSLII*, p. 285n.
31. Ibid., pp. 373, 379.
32. Ibid., pp. 368–9n.
33. Maria Gisborne and Edward E. Williams, *Shelley's Friends, Their Journals and Letters*, F. L. Jones (ed.) (Norman: University of Oklahoma Press, 1951), pp. 121–2, 113–36.
34. Maria Schoina, *Romantic 'Anglo-Italians'* (Farnham: Ashgate, 2009), p. 147.
35. Edward John Trelawny, *Records of Shelley, Byron and the Author* (Harmondsworth: Penguin, 1973), p. 63.
36. *PBSLII*, p. 21n.
37. Ibid., pp. 219, 372.
38. Lucy Hutchinson, *Memoirs of the Life of Colonel Hutchinson* (London: George Bell & Sons, 1906), pp. 84–5.
39. *MWSLI*, p. 93.
40. Mulhallen, *The Theatre of Shelley*, pp. 91, 144.
41. Trelawny, *Records of Shelley*, pp. 142–5.
42. Ibid., p. 106.
43. *MWSLI*, pp. 227–9; Gisborne and Williams, *Shelley's Friends*, pp. 136–8.
44. *MWSLI*, p. 244.
45. Ibid., p. 238
46. *PBSLII*, p. 433.
47. James Bieri, *Percy Bysshe Shelley, A Biography* 2 vols (Newark: University of Delaware Press, 2001), II, p. 320.
48. Trelawny, *Records of Shelley*, pp. 138–9.
49. *PBSLII*, p. 387.
50. Bieri, *Percy Bysshe Shelley*, II, p. 325.

Chapter 6

1. *PBSLII*, p. 371.
2. Ian Birchall, *The Spectre of Babeuf*, p. 167.
3. Eleanor Marx and Edward Aveling, *Shelleys' Socialism and Popular Songs* (London: Journeyman Press, 1979), p. 16.
4. Quoted in Donald Reiman, 'Shelley's Reputation Before 1960', *SPP*, p. 541.
5. Marx and Aveling, *Shelleys' Socialism*, p. 16.
6. Richard Pankhurst, *William Thompson* (London: Pluto Press, 1991), p. 62.
7. Richard Pankhurst, *Sylvia Pankhurst, Artist and Crusader* (London: Paddington Press, 1979), p. 40.
8. Sylvia Pankhurst, *The Suffragette Movement* (London: Virago, 1972), p. 67; I am grateful to Andrew Waterman for information about his mother, Olive Waterman; Howard Zinn, *A People's History of the United States* (Essex: Addison Wesley Longman, 1996), pp. 318–19.
9. Robert Kaufman, *Intervention & Commitment Forever! Shelley in 1819, Shelley in Brecht, Shelley in Adorno, Shelley in Benjamin*, Romantic Circles, www.rc.umd.edu/praxis/interventionist/kaufman/kaufman.html [accessed 17 February 2015].
10. *SPP*, p. 546.
11. 'Shelley's Hellas' adapted by Judith Chernaik, with original music by David Cain, produced and directed by John Theocharis, transmitted BBC Radio 3, 13 June 1976.
12. *OWC*, p. 585.
13. Ibid., p. 670.

Index

Page numbers in italics refer to illustrations

Abernethy, John, 28

Act of Union, *see Parliament*

Address to the People of Ireland
(Theobald Wolfe Tone), 45

Adeline Mowbray (Amelia Opie), 36

Adorno, Theodor W. 131

Aeschylus, 85–6, 116

Africa, 6, 64

Age of Reason (Thomas Paine), 50

Agrarian Justice (Thomas Paine), 67

Agricultural labourers, *see* working
class

Allegra, Claire Clairmont's daughter,
70, 79, 83, 121, 125

America, United States of, 1, 108;
Declaration of Independence,
129; emigration to, 43, 70, 76,
82, 122; 'Rising of the Twenty
Thousand', 131; war in Vietnam,
108; wars with Britain, 8, 10, 43,
49, 97

Amirani, Amir, x

Aristophanes, 109, 111
see also The Frogs

Armagh, Dean of 54

Armstrong, Archibald, 123
see also Charles the First

atheists, atheism, 17, 23, 50, 135

Austria, Emperor of, 124

Babeuf, 'Gracchus', 3, 40, 84, 96, 99,
129

Baillie, James, 7

Bamford, Samuel, 74, 92

bankers and banks, 32, 43, 75, 98, 135

Barclay, Robert, 66

Barnstaple, 49, 50, 51

Barruel, Joseph, 23

Bavaria, 23

Baxter, Robert, 62

Beauclerk, Mrs., 3

Beauty and The Beast, 53

Belfast, 43–4

Benbow, William, 86

Benjamin, Walter, 131

Bentham, Jeremy, 95, 96, 101, 134

Benthamites, 101

Biographie Moderne, 40

Birmingham, 5, 7, 90

Black Dwarf, The (ed. Thomas
Wooler), 71, 82

Blackwood's Edinburgh Magazine, 65

Blake, William, 131

Boinville, Harriet, 59, 61, 62

Bolivar, Byron's boat, 125

Bolton, 89

Bonaparte, Joseph, 27, 81

Bonaparte, Napoleon, 3, 27, 49, 57, 63,
80–1, 128

Brandreth, Jeremiah, 75

Braxfield, Lord, 9

breastfeeding, 61

Brecht, Bertolt, 131

Brian, Havergal, 132

Bristol, 8, 49

British Forum, 31–2, 37

Brockway, Fenner, 131

Brougham, Henry, 89, 104, 105

Browning, Robert, 130

Buonarotti, Filippo, 84

Burdett, Francis, MP, 5, 16, 52, 72, 74, 93, 101; campaigns, 20, 32, 46; dedication by Shelley, 16; discredited, 89; exposure of prison conditions, 5; Hampden Club member, 50; imprisoned, 32, 93; on parliamentary reform 16, 71, 89

Burke, Edmund, 4
   see also Reflections on the French Revolution

Burnley, 89

Bury, 89

Byron, Lord George Gordon Noel, Allegra and, 79, 83, 121, 125; correspondence with Claire Clairmont, 71, 72; correspondence with Shelley, 65, 69; friendship with Shelley, xi, 67–8, 82, 83, 84, 121–2, 127; political views, 67, 81, 82, 89, 105, 108, 117; relationship with Claire, 67, 83, 121, 125; relationship with Teresa Guiccioli, 108, 121; views on Shelley, 84, 122
   see also Childe Harold; Don Juan; Liberal, The

Bysshe, Hellen, 1

Cain, David, 132

Cameron, Kenneth Neill, 58, 131

Canning, George, 105

Cannon, George, 66

Carbonari, 84, 106, 108, 116, 122; Shelley's possible involvement, 84, 122

Carlile, Richard, 71, 91, 94–5, 101, 109, 130

Carlton House, party at, 32–4

Caroline, Queen, wife of George IV, 92, 108–9, 113

Cartwright, Major John, 6, 8, 49–50, 67, 71, 72, 73, 89; on parliamentary reform, 8, 71

Castle, 72, 105
   see also spies

Castlereagh, Lord, 20, 32, 63, 91, 105, 111

Catholic Committee, 43, 44–5, 47–8, 49

Catholic Defenders, 43

Catholic Emancipation, 5, 6, 7, 10, 19, 43, 44, 47, 48, 50, 102

Catholics, Catholicism, 17, 42–3, 46, 48, 122

Cato Street Conspiracy, 94

Cenci, Beatrice, 86–7
   see also Shelley's works, *The Cenci*

Cenci, Count, 86–7
   see also Shelley's works, *The Cenci*

censorship, 8, 50, 71, 72, 77, 87, 114, 117, 121, 124, 135; France, in, 3; Italy, in, 81, 107

Charles I, 50, 73, 97, 122–3
   see also Shelley's works, *Charles the First*

Charles II, 88

Charles the First (Mary Mitford), 124

Chartists, 8; Chartists' Bible, 130

Chernaik, Judith, 132

Cheshire, 42

Chichester, Earl of, 30, 40, 51, 57

Childe Harold (Lord Byron), 67–8

children, abandoned, in Florence and
    Milan, 84
Chinese students, 132
Christian Polity (Thomas Evans), 67
Christians, Christianity, 50, 94, 104
Clairmont, Charles, 36
Clairmont, Jane ('Claire'), 61, 71, 72,
    107, 109, 119; illegitimacy, 36;
    living with Shelley and Mary, 63,
    70, 79, 83; on Byron's views on
    Shelley, 84; relationship with
    Byron, 67, 83, 121, 125;
    relationship with Shelley, 64, 84
Clark, William, 130
Clarke, Robert, 25
Clarkson, Thomas, 6
Cobbett, William, 71, 72, 74, 75, 89,
    100, 134; fled to America, 82;
    imprisoned, 71; on paper money
    and debt, 89, 96; Shelley's views
    on, 96, 98, 101, 105; splits in
    radicals, 72, 89; writing for
    Queen Caroline, 109
    see also Political Register
Cochrane, Lord Thomas, 16, 72, 74
Cold Bath Fields Prison, 5, 67
Coleridge, Samuel Taylor, 40, 53, 106
Combination Acts, *see* Parliament
Compendium of the History of Ireland
    (John Lawless), 47
compositors, *see* working class
Conciliatore, Il, 81
Congress of Vienna, 63, 81, 106
'Conspiracy of Equals', 3, 84
*Constitution of a Perfect
    Commonwealth, The* (Thomas
    Spence), 99
Constitution Society, 9
Continental System, 49, 57
Convention Act, *see* Parliament

Copenhagen Fields, 9
Coplestone, Edward, 19, 24
Corn Law, 1815, *see* Parliament
Cornwall, 7, 49, 100
Cortes, 105
cotton workers, *see* working class
Cromwell, Oliver, 122, 123
    see also Shelley's works, *Charles the
    First*
crises, political and trade, 49, 70–1
    see also Continental System;
    protests
croppers, *see* working class
Cruikshank, George, 93, 109, *110*
'crushers', *see* 'free-thinking'
    community
Cumberland, Richard, 111
Curran, John Philpot, 20, 47
Curran, Sarah, daughter of John
    Philpot, 47
Cuvier, Georges, 17

Dacre, Charlotte, 36
Dawson, P.M.S., xi
Derbyshire, 74
Deists, deism, 48, 50, 61, 94
debt, national, 32, 70, 75, 98, 104, 135
Dionigi, Mariana, 86
Dissenters, 5, 6, 17, 42–3
Don Juan (Lord Byron), 121
Don Juan, Shelley's boat, 125, 126
Don Quixote, 68
Dowden, Edward, 14
Downham Market, 71
du Bois, W.E.B., 131
Duvillard, Elise, 83

Eaton, Daniel Isaac, 50
Ecrasez l'Infame (Voltaire), 36
Edinburgh Review, 19

Edwards, Rev. 'Taffy', 11

Eldon, Lord (John Scott), 9, 19, 69, 91, 111

Eliot, T.S., 131

Ellenborough, Lord, 50

Ellis-Nanney, David, 55–6

Ely, 71

Emmet, Robert, 44, 47

employers, 41–2, 70, 90, 92

  see also yeomanry

Enclosure Acts, *see* Parliament

enclosures, 10, 43, 49, 70

Engels, Friedrich, 130

English Revolution, 97, 99, 123, 133

Enquiry Concerning Political Justice, An (William Godwin), 9, 15, 17, 18, 22, 29

Equiano, Olaudah, 6

Erskine, Thomas, 9

Essay Concerning Human Understanding, An (John Locke), 18, 24

Essay on Slavery (Thomas Clarkson), 6

Essay on the Principle of Population, An (Thomas Malthus), 67

Eton College, 13, 14–15, 21, 28, 120; Shelley's friends, Amos, Andrew, 15; Halliday, Walter S., 15, 17, 25; Leslie, Edward, 14, 17; Tisdall, James, 15, 16; Wellesley, William, 15

Euripides, 21

Evans, Thomas, 67

Examiner, The (ed. Leigh Hunt), 20, 23, 24, 50, 68, 82, 91, 104, 115

Excursion (William Wordsworth), 65

Fables Ancient and Modern (William Godwin), 53

Factory Bill, *see* Parliament

Faerie Queene, The (Edmund Spenser), 96

Fanny, daughter of Mary Wollstonecraft, 36, 60

Field Place, 2, 11

  see also Shelley's travels

Fielding, John, magistrate, 6

Fildes, William, 92

Finnerty, Peter, 20, 44, 45

Fishamble Street Theatre, 48

Fitzgerald, Lord Edward, 3, 20

Foot, Paul, xi, 132

Four Ages of Poetry, The (Thomas Love Peacock), 133

Fournier, 130

Fox, Charles James, 4, 5–6, 9, 10, 15, 32

Foxite Whigs, 6, 9, 129

Frankenstein, (Mary Shelley), xi, 68

France, British reaction to French Revolution, 4–5, 40; constitution, 3, 47, 99, 129; discontent of countries occupied by; 57, 80, 81; French Revolution, 3–5, 17, 92, 99, 101, 128; Irish, support for, 20, 44; wars with, 9, 10, 17, 20, 27–8, 32, 44, 57, 63, 70, 97, 106

  see also Jacobins

'free-thinking' community, 35, 36–7, 54, 63, 119

Frame-breaking Bill, *see* Parliament

framework knitters, *see* working class

Frogs, The (Aristophanes), 109, 116

Fuller, John, 15–16

Gamba, Count Ruggero, 108, 125

Gamba, Pietro, 108, 125

Gandhi, Mahatma, xii, 131

Gellibrand, W.C., 12

General Synod of Ulster, 6

George III, 15, 21, 32, 44

George IV, *see* Prince Regent

Giovanna d'Arco (Salvatore Viganò), 81

Gisborne, John, 82, 86, 87, 88, 109

Gisborne, Maria, 82, 88

Godwin, Mary, *see* Shelley, Mary

Godwin, Mary Jane, 36, 53

Godwin, William, philosopher, 9, 52–3, 61, 74; correspondence with Shelley, 25, 27, 41, 45, 47, 55, 77–8, 88; critical of Shelley, 48; financially supported by Shelley, 53, 58, 62, 106; influence on Shelley, 17; on Mary, 62; on relations between men and women, 35–6; on religion, 19; publishing business, 53; reconciled to Shelley and Mary, 69; rejected Shelley and Mary, 62, 64; sons Charles and William, 53, 59; unsympathetic letters to Mary, 88
    see also Enquiry Concerning Political Justice, An

Goldschmidt, Berthold, 132

Gothic (dir. Ken Russell), 131

Graham, Edward Fergus, 33, 34, 37

Greece, 114–16; independence campaign, 115–16, 119

Grenville, Lord, 19

Grey, Lord Charles, 9

Grove, Charles, 17, 18, 22, 27, 28, 30, 31, 32–3, 35

Grove, Charlotte, 18, 25

Grove, Harriet, 16, 18, 22, 30

Grove, John, 27, 34

Grove, Louisa, 18

Grove, Sir Thomas, 11, 18

Grove, Thomas, 35, 49

Guatimozin, Aztec leader, 105

Guiccioli, Teresa, 108, 121

Habeas Corpus, *see* Parliament

Hampden clubs, 49, 71, 89

Hampden, John, 49–50, 122, 123
    see also Shelley's works, *Charles the First*

Hardy, Thomas, founder of LCS, 4, 6, 9

Hardy, Thomas, novelist and poet, 130

hatters, *see* working class

Haunted Summer (dir. Passer Ivan), 131

Hazlitt, William, 68

Healy, Dan, 45, 47, 49, 51, 55, 61

Helyar, William, 18

Henrietta Maria, Queen, 122
    see also see also Shelley's works, *Charles the First*

Herculaneum, 83

Herschel, William, 15

Hitchener, Elizabeth, 34–5; correspondence with Shelley, 36–7, 40–1, 46, 49; lived with Shelleys, 51, 52; parted from Shelleys, 53–4

Hobhouse, John Cam, 89, 105

Hog's Wash (ed. Daniel Isaac Eaton), 4

Hogg, Thomas Jefferson, 21, 30, 55; atheism, 22–4; correspondence with Shelley, 18, 53, 57; enamoured of Elizabeth Shelley, 34; expulsion from Oxford, 24–5; lived with Shelley, 25–7, 32, 36–7; on marriage, 35; on Shelley, 14, 19, 24, 56, 61, 62; relationship with Harriet Shelley, 37; relationship with Mary Shelley, 64

Holland, 97, 119

Hone, William, 71, 93, 95, 101, 105, 109

Hookham, Thomas, 50, 55

Hooper, Mrs, 49

Horsham, 2, 7, 10, 15–16, 126

hosiers, *see* working class

Huddersfield, 94

Hume, David, 24, 123

Hunt, Henry 'Orator', 8, 68, 70, 72, 82–3, 88, 90, 129; betrayal of working people, 94, 101; legal approach, insistence on, 93–4; on parliamentary reform, 71, 72, 89–90, 94; splits in radicals, 89, 94

Hunt, James Henry Leigh, xi, 23, 65, 113, 121, 125; correspondence with Shelley, 23–4, 42, 65; criticism of Wordsworth, 104; dedication by Shelley, 87; financially supported by Shelley, 68; friendship with Shelley, 31, 38, 68, 70, 121, 126, 127; imprisoned, 50; political agreement with Shelley, 88; publication of Shelley's work, 68, 77, 94–5, 103

see also Examiner, The; Liberal, The

Hunt, John, co-editor of *The Examiner*, 50

Hunt, Marianne, wife of Leigh, 70

Hunt, Thornton, son of Leigh, 38

Hurst, Robert Henry, 7

Hutchinson, Lucy, 123

Illuminati, 23

Imlay, Gilbert, 36

improvvisatori, 114

see also Tommaso Sgricci

India, 3, 69, 100, 119; Kashmir, 64

informers, *see* spies

insurrection, *see* protests

Ireland, 9, 20, 42–5; 1798 Irish Rising, 6, 20, 44, 46, 66, 91

Irwin, Lady, 7, 15

Italy, 80–1, 82, 83–4, 97, 119; Austrians in, 81, 107, 108; Bourbons in, 82, 84; French in, 80; Lucca, 80, 121, 125; Milan, 81, 84; Naples, 80, 81, 83–4, 106–8, 116; Piedmont-Sardinia, 80, 81, 108, 116; Pisa, 115, 119, 121, 122; Rome, 84–5, 127; Sicily, 80, 81, 107; Spezia Gulf of, 125; Venice, 16, 80, 81, 82, 83, 88; Viareggio, 126, 127

see also Shelley's travels

Jacobins, Jacobinism, 3, 67, 80, 81, 83, 84

Jagger, Mick, 131

Jew, The (Richard Cumberland), 111

Jews, Judaism, 50, 80, 94, 111–12

Johnston, James, printer, 114

Jones, Brian, 131

Jones, John Gale, 31–2, 93

Jones, Sir William, 17

Keats, John, 65, 68, 93, 104, 131

Keswick, 41, 56

King Lear (William Shakespeare), 123

La Scala theatre, Milan, 81

labourers, *see* working class

Lake Lucerne, 67

Lamb, Charles and Mary, 53

Lamb, George, 89

Lancashire, 42

Index

Laud, William, Archbishop of
    Canterbury, 122
Lawless, John, 47, 48
Lawrence, William, 28, 38, 79
LCS, *see* London Corresponding
    Society
Leach, Sir John, 111
Leavis, F.R., 131
Leeds Mercury, 75
Leeson, Robert, 54, 55, 57
Leicester, 42
Lenin, Vladimir Ilyich, 73
Levellers, 123
Leveridge, Matthew, 15
Libel Act, *see* Parliament
Liberal, The, 121, 126
Lind, James, 15, 28
Littleport, 71
Liverpool, 8
Liverpool, Lord, 111
Livorno, 106, 109, 115, 126
    see also Shelley's travels
Lleyn Peninsula, 49
Locke, John, 18, 24
London, 20, 30, 41, 48, 67, 71, 72, 74,
    93, 97, 104; City of, 8, 109;
    Tower of, 32, 72
    see also Shelley's travels
London Corresponding Society, xii, 4,
    6, 9, 10, 16, 32, 67, 75
Lowther, Lord, 105–6
Lucca, *see* Italy
Lucas, Timothy Shelley's steward,
    10–11
Lucretius, 15
Ludd, Ned, 42
Luddites, 42, 49, 71
Ludlam, Isaac, 75
Lynmouth, *see* Shelley's travels

Macaulay, Catherine, 123

Macbeth (William Shakespeare), 15
Madocks, William, MP, 16, 52, 54
Mahometan, *see* Muslims
Malthus, Rev. Thomas, 67, 98, 104, 111
Man in the Moon, The (William
    Hone), 93
Manchester, 4, 7, 49, 67, 89, 90, 94; St
    Peter's Fields, 74, 89–90
    see also Peterloo massacre
Manifesto of the Equals (Sylvain
    Maréchal), 40
marches, *see* protests
Maréchal, Sylvain, *Manifesto of the
    Equals*, 40
Marie Antoinette, 4
Marlow, 71
Marx, Eleanor, 130
Marx, Karl, 73, 130
Marxists, Marxism, 130
Masquerade in *The English Dance of
    Death, The* (Thomas
    Rowlandson), 91
Mathews, Charles, 17
Matthews, Geoffrey, 131
Mavrokordatos, Alexandros, 114–15,
    116; influence of Shelley, 116
Maynooth College, 43
McMillan, printer, 77
McNevin, William, 47
Medusa, the, 93
Medwin, Thomas, son of Thomas
    Charles, 10, 11, 14, 15, 16, 17, 38,
    56, 119
Medwin, Thomas Charles, 7, 10, 12,
    15, 35, 58
meetings, public, *see* protests
Merle, W.H., 14
Mexican revolution, 58
Milan, *see* Italy
Milan Commission, 111
Milltown, Earl of, 54

Milton, John, 75
Mitford, Mary, 124
money, paper, 32, 89, 98, 111, 112
Moore, Thomas, 84
Morning Chronicle, 9, 19, 20, 115
Morning Post, 50
Moscow, retreat from, 57, 59
Mountcashell, Lady, 114
Murat, Joseph, 81, 83
Murray, John, 65
Muslims, Islam, xii, 50

Nangtwillt, 49, 62
Naples, *see* Italy
New Shoreham, 7
Newcastle, 67, 94; Philosophical
    Society, 67
Newton, John, 59
Nicaragua, 132
Nicholls, Eleanor, 1
Nicholson, Margaret, 21, *see also*
    Shelley's works, *Posthumous*
    Fragments of Margaret Nicholson
Norfolk, Charles, Duke of, 5–6, 7, 9,
    10, 15, 18–19, 31, 32, 38, 45
Northumberland, Duke of, 16
Norwich, 4, 8
Nottingham, 42, 74
Nugent, Catherine, 47, 49, 50;
    correspondence with Harriet
    Shelley, 53–4, 58, 59, 62, 69

O'Connell, Daniel, 44, 45, 47–8, 102
O'Connell, John, 48
O'Connor, Arthur, 20
O'Neill, Eliza, 87
Oak Apple Day, 88, 123
Observations on the Effect of the
    Manufacturing System (Robert
    Owen), 74

Occupy movement, 132
Oedipus at Colonus (Sophocles), 116
Oedipus Tyrannus (Sophocles), 111
Oliver, 74–5
    see also spies
Ollier, Charles and James, 77, 95, 113,
    116, 117
Opie, Amelia, 36
Orders in Council, *see* Parliament
Orr, William, 20
Owen, Robert, 74, 98, 130
Oxford, 19; University of, 18–19;
    University College, 19–21, 24
Oxford Herald, 20
Oxford University and City Herald, 19

Pacchiani, Professor, 114
Paine, Thomas, 4–5, 19, 45, 67, 94
    see also Age of Reason; Agrarian
    Justice; Rights of Man
Pankhurst, Richard, father of Sylvia
    and Christabel, 130–1
Pankhurst, Sylvia, 131; East London
    Federation of Suffragettes, 131;
    No Conscription Fellowship,
    links to, 131
Parliament and government, Act of
    Union, 44, 47, 48, 112;
    Combination Acts, 41–2, 71;
    Convention Act, 45; Corn Law,
    1815, 70; Enclosure Acts, 70;
    Factory Bill on child working,
    74; Framebreaking Bill, 67;
    Habeas Corpus suspended, 9, 72,
    74, 82; Libel Act, 9; Orders in
    Council, 49; Penal Laws, 42;
    Poyning's Law, 43; prohibition of
    political activity, 10, 74, 90, 94,
    135; Reform Act, 92, 102;
    Seditious Meetings Act, 10, 23,

71, 91, 94; Six Acts, 94; Taxes, 6,
70, 94; Test Acts, 6; Treason Act,
9, 21, 23
see also crises; prosecutions;
protests
parliamentary reform, 6, 8–10, 16, 67,
71, 93; alternative
representative, 90; divisions
among reformers, 71–2, 73, 89,
93–4; revival of agitation, 102;
suffrage demands, 72, 73, 102
see also crises; Parliament;
parliamentary representation;
protests
parliamentary representation, 4–5, 7,
8–9, 15, 100, 111; 'rotten
boroughs', 7, 99, 111
Passer, Ivan, 131
Peacock, Thomas Love, agent for
Shelley, 95; correspondence
with Shelley, 66, 82, 89, 96, 106;
friendship with Shelley, 55, 59,
64, 70; on Shelley's marriage,
61; on poetry, 77, 86, 96, 133–4;
on Shelley, 56, 63, 66, 77, 96,
130; sent Shelley journals, 82–3,
91
Pellico, Silvio, 81
Penal Laws, *see* Parliament
Persians, The (Aeschylus), 116
Peter Bell (William Wordsworth), 104
Peter Bell, A Lyrical Ballad (J.H.
Reynolds), 104
Peterloo Massacre, 70, 88–91, 103;
effects, 91–4
petitions, *see* protests
Phillips, C & W, printers, 17, 23
Phillips, James, 7
Picasso, Pablo, 86

Pieces of Irish History (William
McNevin), 47
Piedmont-Sardinia, *see* Italy
Pig's Meat (ed. Spence, Thomas), 4, 67
Pilfold, Captain John, 18, 34
Pisa, *see* Italy
Pitt, William, 4, 7, 8, 15, 44
Place, Francis, 16
*Plan of Parliamentary Reform in the
Form of a Catechism* (Jeremy
Bentham), 95
Plato, 21, 86
Pliny, 15
Plutarch, 21
Poe, Edgar Allen, 130
Poland, 119, 133
Political House that Jack Built, The
(William Hone), 93
*Political Justice, see Enquiry Concerning
Political Justice, An*
Political Register (ed. William
Cobbett), 32, 71, 82, 89
Poll Tax campaigners, 132
Pompeii, 83, 108
Pope, Dr. Robert, 66
Portugal, 27–8
poverty, 70–1
Poyning's Law, *see* Parliament
Press, The, 20, 45
Preston, 8
Price, Richard, 4
Priestley, Joseph, 5
Priestman, Martin, 23
Prince Regent, later George IV, 10, 32,
33, 34, 50, 72, 89, 109, 111
Princess Charlotte, 75
Prometeo (Salvatore Viganò), 81
Prometheus Bound (Aeschylus), 85
prosecutions and trials, political, 9,
32, 42, 45, 50, 71, 74–5, 94, 114

Protestant Ascendancy, 42, 44, 54
Protestants, Protestantism, 42–3, 46, 122
protests, demonstrations, 9, 71–2, 93; failure of legal action, 94; insurrection, 74, 99, 101; machine-breaking, 42; marches, 74; meetings and 'free and easies', 9, 67, 70, 71, 90, 93, 94; petitioning Parliament, 6, 8, 41, 44–5, 49–50, 67, 72; petitioning the Prince Regent, 89; rebellion, 71; revolutions, 119; riots for parliamentary reform, 72; riots over enclosures, 49; riots over food prices, 9, 42, 49, 71; strikes, 52, 94, 131, 132; strikes of cotton spinners, 41, 70, 89; strikes of tin miners, 49; strikes of weavers, 89; tax boycott, 70 *see also* Luddites; France
Puritans, Puritanism, 122, 123
  see also Shelley's works, *Charles the First*
Pym, John, 123
  see also Shelley's works, *Charles the First*

Quakers, Quakerism, 6–7, 46, 66, 92, 128
Quarterly Review, The, x, 40, 65, 86, 121
quarrymen, *see* working class
Queen's Matrimonial Ladder, The (William Hone), 109, 110

radicals, 8, 17, 28, 31, 59, 71, 94, 108–9
  see also individuals
Real Rights of Man (Thomas Spence), 67

rebellion, *see* protests
Recollections of the Last Days of Byron and Shelley (Edward John Trelawny), 124
Records of Shelley, Byron and the Author (Edward John Trelawny), 124
Red Shelley (Paul Foot), 132
Reeve Bloor, Ella, 131
Reflections on the French Revolution (Edmund Burke), 4, 5, 17
Reform Bill and Act, *see* Parliament
Reformist, The, 71
Rejected Addresses (Horace Smith), 68
Rennie, John, 12
Republican, The, formerly *Sherwin's Political Register*, 95
Reveley, Henry, 106
Reynolds, J.H., 104
Ricardo, David, 111
Rights of Man (Thomas Paine), 4–5, 29, 44, 67
riots, *see* protests
Roberts, Captain, 125, 126
Roe, James, 21, 25
Rolling Stones, 131
Rossetti, William, 69
'rotten boroughs', *see* parliamentary representation
Rousseau, Jean-Jacques, 75
Rowan, Hamilton, 47
Rowlandson, Thomas, 91
Russell, Ken, 131
Russian Revolution, 92, 133

San Giuliano Terme, *see* Shelley's travels
Sandinistas, 132
Scotland, Convention of Scottish reformers, 9, 43; Highland

clearances, 70; Scottish Kirk, 122

Scott, John, *see* Eldon, Lord

Scottish Convention, *see* Scotland

Scrivener, Michael, xi

Second World War, 59

Seditious Meetings Act, *see* Parliament

Sergison, Colonel, 12, 15–16, 18

sex, oral, 21

Sgricci, Tommaso, 107, 114

Shackleton, Dr. Abraham, 66

Shakespeare, William, *see* *King Lear*, *Macbeth*

Sharpe, Charles Kirkpatrick, 22, 24

Shaw, George Bernard, 131

Sheffield, 4, 67

Shelley, Bysshe, grandfather, 1

Shelley, Charles, son by Harriet, 59, 63, 69

Shelley, Clara, daughter by Mary, 70, 83

Shelley, Elena, adopted daughter, 84, 106

Shelley, Eliza Ianthe, daughter by Harriet, 55, 56, 57, 61, 62, 69

Shelley, Elizabeth, mother, 10, 11, 37

Shelley, Elizabeth, sister, 14, 16, 17, 18, 22, 30, 34, 37, 52, 54

Shelley, Harriet (Westbrook), x, 30–1, 37, 42, 45, 49, 52, 53–4, 55, 56, 58; allowance and custody battle, 68; appearance, 30, 54; character, 36, 38, 60–1; children, *see* Shelley, Eliza Ianthe *and* Shelley, Charles; elopement and marriage, 35, 36, 59; estrangement and separation from Shelley, 53–4, 59–63,

69–70; letters from Shelley, 69; suicide, 69

Shelley, Hellen, sister, 11, 17, 18, 36

Shelley, Mary, sister, 30

Shelley, Mary (Godwin), x, xi, 14, 36, 62, 65, 66, 67, 68, 71, 81–2, 83, 106–7, 119, 124, 127; appearance, 62; character, 62, 63, 64; health, 64, 83, 88, 106, 125; marriage, 69; meeting and elopement, 62, 63; incompatibility with Claire Clairmont, 64; jealousy of Harriet Shelley, 63; on Cobbett, 100; on Shelley, 103, 114; open marriage, 62, 64, 114; published Shelley's collected works, 130

Shelley, Percy Bysshe
  activism, 16, 25, 32–4, 45–7, 48–9, 51, 54–5, 130; anonymity, use of 22, 23, 25; appearance, 12, 25, 39, 68; Associations, 47–9; atheism, 15, 17, 18, 19, 22–6, 31, 62, 68, 69, 77, 94, 135; attacks, literary, 131; attacks, physical, 55–7, 125; boating, 12, 15, 64, 70, 119, 121, 124–5, 126; bullied, allegedly, 14; character, x–xi, 1, 10–11, 12, 14–15, 21, 25, 30, 31, 37–40, 41, 45, 55–6, 57, 65, 66, 68, 103, 122, 126, 128; childhood, 10–18; custody battle, 9, 68–9; death, 126–7; debts, 38, 39–40, 55, 58, 59, 62, 63–4, 79; education, *see* Edwards, Rev. 'Taffy'; Syon House; Eton College; Oxford; expulsion from university, 24–5; father, relations with, *see* Shelley, Timothy; generosity, 10–11, 45–6, 55, 71, *see also*

support; health, 12, 22, 26, 28,
37, 38, 55–6, 63, 66, 70, 79, 84,
88, 106, 121, 125–6; income, 27,
29, 34, 37, 38, 45, 55, 63–4, 68,
79; influences on his ideas,
xi–xii, 15, 16, 17, 21, 28–9, 31,
35–6, 40, 44, 45, 47, 55, 59,
65–7, 73, 74, 81–2, 83, 86, 96,
98, 99, 102, 129; inheritance and
rank, 1–2, 29–30, 35, 54, 58;
injustice, opposition to, 11, 17;
medical career, 27–9, 38;
memory, excellent, 10, 12;
parliamentary career, 19, 24, 25,
31; plays performed and adapted,
132–3; pranks, 11–12, 14, 23;
quoted widely, 130–2; reading,
reading aloud, 12, 14, 15, 21, 55,
86, 123; relationships, *see
individuals*; science, 11, 12, 15,
21, 106; shooting, 15, 22, 55–6,
84, 121–2, 125; sisters,
relationship with, 11, 14, 16, 17,
22, 27, 29–30, 34, 37; support for
commercial projects, 52, 53, 55,
58, 106; support for political
campaigners, 20, 23, 42, 50,
94–5, 105, 115; theatre, 12, 15;
vegetarianism, 10, 59, 131;
writing career, 11, 12, 14, 15, 19,
32, 61, 65, 66, 88, 122, 130, *see
also Liberal, The*; writing style,
58, 85–6
Shelley's travels
England, Bishopsgate, 64;
Bracknell, 59, 62; Cuckfield, 34;
Field Place, 1–2, 10–12, 15,
16–18, 22, 33, 34, 37; Lake
District (including Keswick), 37,
38–41, 59; Lechlade, 64;

London, 16, 17, 26–34, 35, 52, 57,
62, 63, 69; Lynmouth, 49–51;
Marlow, 70; Oxford, 18–25;
Wiltshire, 11; York, 37
Ireland (including Dublin), 45–9,
55, 57
Italy, Florence, 106, 114; Lerici,
125, 126; Milan, 81; Naples, 83;
Piedmont, 81; Livorno, 82, 88,
119, 121; Pisa, 106, 114, 119, 121;
Ravenna, 121; Rome, 84–6; San
Giuliano Terme, 109, 119;
Venice, 82, 83
Rhine, the, 63
Scotland, 35; Edinburgh, 37, 59
Switzerland (including Geneva),
63, 67–8
Wales, 35, 49, 52, 54–5; Tremadog,
52, 54–5
Shelley's views
on aristocracy, 98–9, 135; on
Byron, 122; on Bysshe Shelley, 1;
on education, 97, 98, 100, 103;
on the English, 86, 112, 117–19;
on equality, 30, 96–9, 102, 134;
on Greek independence, 116–17;
on Greek theatre, 116; on incest,
76, 86–7; on Ireland, 45–8; on
Italians, 82, 86, 97, 108; on Jews,
111–12; on liberty, 75–7, 85,
92–3, 97, 99, 113, 116–17, 133,
135; on marriage, 22, 35–6, 69;
on monarchy, tyranny and
Bonaparte, 21–2, 46, 48, 51,
57–8, 73, 75–6, 82, 85, 87–8,
91–3, 97, 99, 101, 107, 108, 109,
111, 116–17, 123–4; on money,
wealth and economics, 97–8,
103, 104–5, 112, 134–5; on
Naples and Sicily, 107–8; on

parliamentary reform, 98–102, 134; on poetry, 64–5, 96, 103, 104–5, 133–4, 135; on politics, xii, 16, 21–4, 29, 34–5, 42, 46–8, 50–1, 57–8, 72–6, 87, 89, 91–3, 99–103, 116–17, 122–4; on religion, xii, 22, 46–8, 50, 61–2, 91, 94, 97, 98, 99, 104, 111, 117, 135; on revolution, xi, 34, 73, 76–7, 84–5, 87, 91–3, 99–102, 107–8, 113, 117–19, 128–9, 133; on violence and war, xii, 21–2, 28, 46, 58, 76–7, 84–5, 87, 91–2, 97, 100–2, 116–17; on women, 1, 11, 27, 37, 69, 75, 76–7, 86, 87–8, 99, 107; on the working class, xi, 34, 41–2, 45–6, 54, 59, 75, 85, 91–3, 97–9, 101–2, 108, 123–4, 129, 134–5

Shelley's works

  Address to the Irish People, 45–7, 54–5; *Address to the People on the Death of the Princess Charlotte*, 75–6; *Adonaïs*, 131; *Alastor, or the Spirit of Solitude*, 64–5, 76; 'Ballad of the Starving Mother', 103, 104; *Boat on the Serchio, The*, 119; *Cenci, The*, 87–8, 95, 124, 132; *Charles the First*, 122–4; *Declaration of Rights*, 47, 49, 51, 54–5, 95, 99, 130; *Defence of Poetry, A*, 29, 133, 135; *Devil's Walk, The*, 51; 'England in 1819', 103; *Esdaile Notebook, The*, 55, 58; 'Feelings of a Republican on the Fall of Napoleon', 57–8; *Hellas*, 116–17, 118, 132, 134; *Hymn to Intellectual Beauty*, 68; 'Irishman's Song, The', 16; *Julian and Maddalo*, 88; *Laon and*

  Cythna (The Revolt of Islam), 70, 76–9, 78, 117, 130–1; *Letter to Lord Ellenborough, A*, 50; 'Lines Written during the Castlereagh Administration', 103; *Lines Written in the Euganean Hills*, 83; 'Love's Philosophy', 95; *Mask of Anarchy, The*, 76, 91–3, 94, 103, 105, 131, 132; minor poems, *see Esdaile Notebook, The*; *Mont Blanc*, 68; *Necessity of Atheism, The*, 22–5, 50, 95; 'New National Anthem, A', 103; *Ode to Naples*, 83, 108, 109; *Ode to the West Wind*, 77, 83; *On a Future State*, 28; *On a Vegetable Diet*, 59; *On Life*, 28, 128; 'On Robert Emmet's Tomb', 50; *On the Game Laws*, 34–5, 70; *Ozymandias*, 68, 132; *Peter Bell the Third*, 104–5; *Philosophical View of Reform, A*, 34, 77, 92, 93, 95–102, 103, 113, 123, 128–9, 133–4; *Poetical Essay on the Existing State of Things, A*, 20; popular songs, volume of, 96, 103; *Posthumous Fragments of Margaret Nicholson*, 21–2; *Prometheus Unbound*, 29, 83, 84–6, 91, 133; *Proposal for Putting Reform to the Vote, A*, 72–4, 97; *Proposals for an Association of Philanthropists*, 46–7, 54; *Queen Mab*, 52, 55, 57, 58–9, 60, 66, 69, 93, 130; *Refutation of Deism, A*, 28, 61–2, 72; *Revolt of Islam, The, see Laon and Cythna*; *Rosalind and Helen*, 87, 119; 'Song to the Men of England', 103; *St. Irvyne*, 17, 18, 22, 36; *Swellfoot the Tyrant*,

109–14, 132–3, 135; *Symposium* (translation), 86; 'Tale of Society as it is, A', 58; 'To Liberty', 58; 'To the Republicans of North America', 58; 'To Sidmouth and Castlereagh', 103; *Triumph of Life, The*, 126; *Victor and Cazire* (with Elizabeth Shelley), 15, 16, 17, 18, 21; *Wandering Jew, The*, 16, 17; 'What Men Gain Fairly', 103; *Zastrozzi*, 16–17

Shelley, Percy Florence, son by Mary, 106

Shelley, Timothy, father, 1–2, 20, 22; approval of Shelley's writing, 17, 19, 20; character, 17, 27, 37; opposition to Shelley's opinions, 25, 26–7, 29–30, 34, 35, 37, 58, 130; political career, 5–6, 7

Shelley, William, son by Mary, 64, 83, 88

Sheridan, Richard Brinsley, 5–6, 9, 20, 32

Sherwin's Political Register, later *The Republican*, 71, 89, 91

shoemakers, *see* working class

Sicily, *see* Italy

Sidmouth, Lord, 90, 91

Sinn Fein, 90

Six Acts, *see* Parliament

Slatter and Munday, bookseller, 19, 23

Slave trade, 6–7, 15–16, 91; opposition to, 6–7, 15–16; parliamentary division, 7

Smith, Adam, 111

Smith, Horace, 68, 70, 98, 113–14; financial advisor to Shelley, 68; moved to Pisa, 121

Smithfield, 70, 93

Socialist Workers Party, Marxism conference, 132

Society for the Suppression of Vice, 114

Society of Friends, *see* Quakers

Soldier's Friend (William Cobbett), 71

soldiers, action of, 90–1, 92, 113; government use of, 42, 90–1, 100, 101, 125; workers' attitude to, 72

Somerset, James, 6

Sophocles, 111, 116

Southey, Robert, 40–1, 65, 105

Spa Fields, 72

Spain and its colonies, 27–8, 81, 106

Spence, Thomas, 66–7, 96; on parliamentary reform, 67; *see also Pig's Meat*

Spenceans, 66–7, 71–2, 93, 94; on parliamentary reform, 71

Spenser, Edmund, 96

Spezia, Gulf of, *see* Italy

spies, informers and co-operators, government, 5, 20, 44, 45, 49, 50, 57, 72, 74–5, 100, 105, 109, 111, 112

spinners, *see* working class

St. Bartholomew's Hospital, 27, 28

Stacey, Sophia, 114

Stalin, Josef, 86

Stanhope, Lord, 50

steamboats, 106

stockbrokers, the Stock Exchange, 32, 68, 98, 135

Stockdale, J.J., London publisher, 22

Stockdale, John, Dublin printer, 20, 45

Stop the War Coalition, x, xii

Swift, Jonathan

Swinburne, Algernon Charles, 130

Swiss Family Robinson (The Family Robinson Crusoe) (Johann David Wyss), 53
Syle, printer, 50
Symposium (Plato), 86
Syon House, 11, 12, 14, 126

tailors, *see* working class
Tales from Shakespear (Charles and Mary Lamb), 53
Tanyrallt, 54–5
Taxes, *see* Parliament
Tennyson, Alfred, 130
Test Acts, *see* Parliament
Theatre in England, 87
Theatre Royal, Covent Garden, 87, 124
Theatre Royal, Drury Lane, 87, 111
Theocaris, John, 132
Theological Inquirer (ed. George Cannon), 66
Thistlewood, Arthur, 94
Thompson, E.P., 90
Thompson, William, 48, 130–1
Thorndike, Sybil, later Dame, 87, 132
Tiananmen Square, 132
Tighe, George, 114
Times, The, 91
tin miners, *see* working class
Tone, Theobald Wolfe, 20, 45
Tories, 4, 89, 102, 105
trades clubs, 101
  see also unions
Traeth Mawr, 52
Trelawny, Edward John, 124, 125, 127; on Shelley, 124–5, 126
Tremadog, 49, 52, 53
  see also Shelley's travels
trials, *see* prosecutions
Tribune of the People (ed. 'Gracchus' Babeuf), 3

Trotsky, Leon, 129
Truro, 49
Turner, William, 75
Tyas, John, 91

unions, 41, 89, 90
  see also Parliament, Combination Acts
United Irishmen, xii, 3, 20, 23, 43–4, 47
University College, *see* Oxford
Utopian socialists, Utopian socialism, 130

Vane, the younger, Sir Henry, 123
  see also Shelley's works, *Charles the First*
Vesuvius, 83
Vienna, Congress of, *see* Congress of Vienna
Viganò, Salvatore, 81–2, 86, 123
Vince, Mrs., 68
Vindication of the Rights of Woman, A (Mary Wollstonecraft), 2, 4
'vitality debate', 28
Vivian, Charles, 126
Viviani, Teresa, 114
Volney, Comte de, Constantin-François, *Ruins of Empire*, 59
Voltaire (Jean-Francois Arouet), *see also Ecrasez l'Infame*, 75

'Walcheren disaster', 20, 31–2
Walker, Adam, 12, 15
Walker, Rev. John, 24
Washington, George, 10
Waterman, Olive, 131
Watson, 'young', 72, 93
We Are Many, (dir. Amirani, Amir), x
weavers, *see* working class

Wedgwood, Josiah, 6
Weekly Messenger, 48
Wellington, Duke of (Arthur Wellesley), 28, 57, 111
Westbrook, John, Harriet's father, 30, 38
Westbrook, Eliza, 30–1, 35, 37, 38, 42, 45, 46, 49, 52, 53, 57, 58, 61
Westbrook, Harriet, *see* Shelley, Harriet
Westminster, 8, 16; elections, 89
Westminster Committee, 8, 71, 89, 93
Wheeler, Anna, 130
Whigs, 4, 5–6, 8, 9, 19, 30, 71, 94, 102
Whitaker, Mr., composer, 53
Whiteboys, 43
Whitton, William, 27, 29–30, 38
Wilberforce, William, 7
Williams, Edward, 119, 124; boating with Shelley, 119; on Byron's views on Shelley, 122
Williams, Jane (Cleveland), 119; character, 119, 126; children, Edward and Rosalind, 119; effect on Shelley, 119, 126; views on Shelley, 124
Williams, John, 52, 54–5, 56, 57
Wollstonecraft, Mary, 2, 4, 36, 40, 123
Wolseley, Sir Charles, 90

Women, position in society of, 1–2, 11, 36, 68, 69–70, 86; suffragists, 8, 130–1; support for Queen Caroline, 109
Wood, Matthew, MP, 109
Wooler, Thomas, 101
Wordsworth, William, 40, 65, 104–5
working class, 41, 70–1, 74, 90; Ireland, in, 43, 44; poetry and, 85–6, 92; theatre and, 87
  trades, agricultural workers, 41; children, 74; compositors, 41; cotton workers, 32, 74; croppers (cloth finishers), 42; framework knitters, 41, 74; hatters, 41; hosiers, 41–2; labourers, 74; quarrymen, 74; shoemakers, 41, 101; spinners, 41, 70–1, 89; tailors, 41; weavers, 41, 50, 89 *see also* protests, trades clubs, unions
Wyss, Johann David, 53

yeomanry, 90–1, 92, 94
Yorke, Charles Philip, 31
Yorkshire, 42, 100; Lord Lieutenant of, 94

Zephaniah, Benjamin, 132

15703053R00113

Printed in Great Britain
by Amazon